The Mindful Path
Through Anxiety

The
Mindful Path
Through Anxiety

AN 8-WEEK PLAN TO
QUIET YOUR MIND & GAIN CALM

TANYA J. PETERSON, MS, NCC

ROCKRIDGE
PRESS

For general information on our other products and services or to obtain technical support, please contact our Customer Care Department within the United States at (866) 744-2665, or outside the United States at (510) 253-0500.

Rockridge Press publishes its books in a variety of electronic and print formats. Some content that appears in print may not be available in electronic books, and vice versa.

Interior and Cover Designer: Michael Cook
Art Producer: Samantha Ulban
Editor: Meera Pal
Production Editor: Jenna Dutton

All images used under license © Shutterstock
Author photo courtesy of © Shanna Chess

ISBN: Print 978-1-64739-299-4 | eBook 978-1-64739-300-7
R0

To my family.

You give me joy and happiness.
You are my motivation to be mindful
of all my moments.
You contribute greatly to my
quality life—without anxiety—and
I'm grateful to all of you.

Contents

Introduction

When I was a young child, I didn't have an imaginary friend. I had an imaginary enemy. Only it wasn't all that imaginary. It was very real, and it was big. It didn't even have a name. It was this vague, indescribable, negatively opinionated companion. It told me to worry about what I said and did—and what others thought of me. It also made me worry that I'd never be good enough for anything if I wasn't absolutely perfect. It went to school with me when I entered kindergarten and stayed with me through college and back to school again when I was a high school teacher and, later, a counselor. It hung out with me in all facets of my life for a long time, and it grew much bigger after I sustained a traumatic brain injury (TBI) in a car accident when my kids were young. By then, I knew its name: anxiety (especially social anxiety and performance anxiety). It wasn't until I came to know and understand anxiety that I finally discovered how to undo the knots that this enemy tangled me in, and to live my life fully and freely.

I offer you this book as someone who has lived with anxiety and overcome it. (Truthfully, anxiety rears its ugly head in everyone's life from time to time, including mine, but now I know how to untangle it and replace it with better things.) I've experienced anxiety myself; I've worked with a few therapists for my anxiety—including some in a behavioral health hospital after my TBI. I helped my students with anxiety. I also earned a master's degree in counseling and am a board-certified counselor (although I'm not currently in practice as I work to reach people through my books and online articles), and I read a lot of research about anxiety and transcending it. It's from this background—plus my hodgepodge of rich life experiences—that I present to you *The Mindful Path Through Anxiety: An 8-Week Plan to Quiet Your Mind & Gain Calm*.

As you work through this book, you can expect to grow. The book you're holding in your hands is different from other anxiety and mindfulness books. *The Mindful Path Through Anxiety* will help you truly understand anxiety and how it impacts your life. It's hard to sort through anxiety and truly move past it into your quality life if you just try to walk over the surface, ignoring the heart of it. That said, you don't want to get stuck in trying to understand anxiety and its workings in your life. Like everyone, including me, you need practical and active ways to overcome it. You'll discover many exercises designed to help you do just that.

Mindfulness is a key component of this book, too. Mindfulness is a powerful way to live life. More than just a tool or technique, it's a mind-set. In this book, you'll explore and discover mindfulness in useable ways that apply to overcoming anxiety, and you'll be able to live mindfully long after you turn the last page. I embrace mindfulness in my life, and I live it happily and peacefully. I'm grateful that you've chosen this book so I can share my knowledge and experiences with you, and you can untangle your own anxiety and live your quality life, too. Let's go!

How to Use This Book

Your first important task in using this book is to celebrate your choice to move out of anxiety's grasp and the personal power that comes with that choice. And I do mean celebrate! The act of celebrating tells the brain that it did something good or is part of something good. Celebrations are as simple as taking a quick break to actively notice something positive, such as making a great decision to embark on an eight-week journey to untangle your anxiety. Purposefully celebrating, even in small ways, like taking a moment to mindfully savor a sip of tea or do a quick happy dance, boosts self-confidence, enhances motivation, and fosters a genuine can-do spirit that catapults you toward more success. How? Science tells us that celebrating releases dopamine, the feel-good neurochemical that is the brain's confetti or colorful cascade of balloons.

It's the *act* of celebrating, not just thinking about it, that leads to action, results, and more action. That is just like your choice to pick up and complete this book. You will be engaged, learning, and doing things over the next eight weeks that will allow you to untangle your anxiety. Here's how you can use this book to maximize your personal success in reducing anxiety and learning to live mindfully:

Adopt an open mind-set. My purpose in writing this book is to guide readers through learning. You'll learn a lot about anxiety so you can understand it and its impact on you. You'll also learn mindfulness as a way of being that will come to replace an anxious way of living. Quite likely, you already have an open mind for learning. Anxiety gets in the way of that, though, by taking information and twisting it and turning it against you. When you notice yourself saying things like "That's so obvious; I should have known that," or "Why do I do X or think Y?" stop and remind yourself that this information isn't there to judge you or make you berate yourself. Anxiety will want to stay in control by distracting you from learning and doing. Pull away from worries and fears by being open to the information without interpreting it through anxiety's lens. Befriend yourself with an open mind on this journey!

Make a commitment, a promise to yourself. I decided to structure this book as an eight-week journey. I did that on purpose, to help you pace yourself in a way that is neither too slow (as in completing a chapter and putting the book aside for months before opening the next—I've done that when reading books, even books I really like, and it's not as effective as reading straight through) nor too fast (speeding through it without letting the information and exercises sink in and become part of you). The structured journey begins in chapter 2.

Chapter 1 dives into vital information about anxiety and mindfulness that will help you along the rest of the path. Read the first chapter at your own pace, and then consider devoting one week to each subsequent chapter. In any given week, however, take the time you need to learn in a meaningful and practical way. Whether you adopt this pace or decide to go a little faster or slower according to your preferences, make a promise to yourself to commit to spending some time every day to untangle your anxiety and dance free from it.

A helpful hint: Turn your book time into a pleasant, inviting ritual. Dedicate a comfortable space, use a favorite pen, light a candle or turn on an essential-oil diffuser, and sip a cup of tea while you work.

Take dedicated action and work it! I've structured the book so it's easy to follow, but with anxiety, there's no such thing as an "easy" button that fixes everything with a single whack. Anxiety ties strong, convoluted, and disorganized knots around us that aren't easy to untangle. (Have you ever tried to undo a hard, tight little knot in a shoelace that's cold, wet, and muddy?) While I can't promise that you're going to overcome your anxiety completely in eight weeks, this book will teach you strategies to untangle and manage it.

You'll be doing exercises throughout the book as well as learning how to use mindfulness for a calm, quality life. With dedication, work, commitment, and your open mind-set, you've got this. This book is a guide, and you can actively put it to use to empower yourself.

I'm confident that you're ready to take back your life! Turn the page, and let's begin!

 Another helpful hint: You'll need a notebook to really make your work successful. Use a special one dedicated just for your journey, and even decorate it if you want to. As you read, I'll prompt you when to use it.

*If you want to make peace
with your enemy, you have to work
with your enemy.
Then he becomes your partner.*

—Nelson Mandela

CHAPTER ONE

Unraveling Anxiety and Mindfulness

This chapter paves the road for your journey ahead. You'll learn the official definition of anxiety and explore its many nuances—including its many forms and how it affects us. It's only when you know and understand anxiety that you can truly work with it to untangle it. It is through knowledge and work that you find your peace.

Similarly, to make genuine, comfortable peace with not only your enemies but also your friends, you need to know and be active with them, too. This chapter is the beginning of your path to befriending mindfulness, and it begins with understanding. We'll cover why mindfulness is effective in helping people with anxiety and include ways you can personalize it to make it fit you naturally.

So settle into your space and prepare to enjoy the ride of your (quality) life!

Understanding Anxiety

Anxiety isn't fictional. Scientists and medical and mental-health professionals have identified and described it. The American Psychiatric Association officially defines it in the *Diagnostic and Statistical Manual of Mental Disorders, Fifth Edition* (DSM-5) as "excessive fear and anxiety [worry] and related behavioral disturbances."

While the DSM-5 definition reassures us that anxiety is real, it doesn't do much to clarify what we're facing. Deeper understanding comes from leaving the textbook and planting ourselves in the world. To do that, let's peek into a moment in Evonne's day when anxiety turns a mundane trip to the grocery store into a problematic ordeal.

Needing something for dinner, Evonne heads to the store after work. Preoccupied with worries about her mistakes of the day, she wanders the aisles. Berating herself for her lack of focus, she heads to the freezer section. New thoughts pop into her mind: "I'm a horrible mother. I should be making something fresh. I'm hurting my kids." She hears someone say, "Excuse me," and realizes she's blocking the freezer door. She feels her face redden with embarrassment and, without making eye contact with the person, she hurries out of the aisle. Upset and unable to think clearly about what to make for dinner, Evonne decides to just grab fast food on the way home. She worries about the expense and the lack of nutrition, but she is at a loss for what else to do. Frustrated, she wonders why she can't just feed her family like a "normal person."

Evonne's anxiety might not have been visible to an observer, but underneath the exterior, a lot was happening.

Anxiety and Your Body

Anxiety is a whole-body ordeal. Evonne's worries activated her sympathetic nervous system, which directs the body's involuntary response to dangerous or stressful situations. Her heart rate quickened, her blood pressure rose, her breathing became more rapid and shallow, and her face became flushed. She might have also experienced muscle tension, chest pain, dizziness, headache, nausea, and shakiness. Later, her parasympathetic nervous system—which slows the body's heart rate and breathing, and returns blood supply to vital digestive organs—will kick in. When it does, she will feel crushing fatigue.

Anxiety and Your Brain

Researchers using fMRI technology, which measures small changes in blood flow that occur with brain activity, have found solid evidence of the brain's extensive role in anxiety. Every area of your brain reacts to anxiety triggers. Evonne's brain was already in overdrive as she ruminated about

her workday, and the neurological response escalated when s
shop for dinner.

Her brain signaled the release of stress hormones such
adrenaline, and norepinephrine. Her prefrontal cortex, the area at the
front of the brain related to thinking, planning, and executive functioning, kept her thoughts stuck in worries and was responsible for
her lack of concentration. Her limbic system, an important emotional
center within the brain, generated irritation, frustration, and embarrassment. The reptilian area of her brain, responsible for the fight-or-flight
instinct, drove her out of the store. Structures within the brain, such as
the amygdala, hypothalamic-pituitary-adrenal (HPA) axis, hippocampus,
and lateral septum, plus hormones and neurotransmitters (messengers of
neurologic information from one cell to another), kept Evonne—and keep
you—mired in anxiety.

When Anxiety Gets in the Way

Anxiety becomes a problem when our brain and body overreact to what
we think are threats. When anxiety impacts thoughts, emotions, and
behaviors, it causes distress and discomfort, consumes mental and physical energy, and limits our full participation in various areas of life. It can
keep us from enjoying our family and friends, performing well at school
or work, and being able to relax and experience joy.

Ordinary daily life becomes a struggle when anxiety winds its way
around and through our very being. Anxiety involves your brain and body,
but it is not your brain or body. In this book, you'll untangle your anxiety
and learn to override it with mindfulness. Fear and worry won't continue
to interfere with the real you and how you live your life.

Anxiety vs. Fear

In defining anxiety, the DSM-5 lumps fear and anxiety together in the same sentence yet distinguishes them as separate words. That's because both seize our thoughts and emotions and affect our behavior. Fear and anxiety negatively impact us in similar ways. They're not identical, however. Each has a unique foundation and focus.

Fear is concrete. It's a response to an imminent threat, something that is happening right now. Fear is present-focused. Fear is often rational because there is tangible evidence of a threat. If you're driving on a busy street and a car runs a stop sign, almost hitting you, you will probably feel a surge of fear that will flood your thoughts and emotions. That's a rational response to a situation. In some cases, however, fear is irrational. If you have a phobia of snakes and a small, harmless one slithers across your path, your fear response will be strong. It's illogical but still present-focused. Whether rational or irrational, fear is external to you.

In contrast to fear, anxiety is focused anywhere but the present. It involves ruminations and regrets about the past or worries about what might happen in the near or distant future. While anxiety feels very real to you, there is nothing tangible to explain it. Despite how it may feel, it doesn't involve situations themselves but instead has to do with your thoughts and feelings about a past or future situation. Anxiety is an internal experience.

Both fear and anxiety affect what you think, how you feel, and how you act in your life. Happily, you can reduce the impact of both.

Forms of Anxiety

"Anxiety" is a broad term. Everyone who lives with it experiences worries and/or fears that affect what they think, feel, and do, and, by extension, limit their life in many ways. That said, anxiety is a very personal experience that takes different forms. All anxiety involves worry, ruminating (agonizing over thoughts and situations repeatedly in your mind), anticipating something upsetting, and reacting to real and imagined dangers. It is the situation or object of worry that differs among the types of anxiety. Perhaps you will recognize your own anxiety among these common forms.

Generalized Anxiety

Generalized anxiety is nonspecific, but don't let its vague nature fool you. If you suffer from this type of anxiety, your negative thoughts and emotions are very clear; it's just that they are all over the place, rather than homed in on one topic. Generalized anxiety is boundless worry—excessive concern about many different things at once.

Not only are these worries numerous, they are much stronger than ordinary concerns. Nearly all parents, for example, worry about their children's safety, but a parent with generalized anxiety might worry so much that they overprotect the children to the detriment of their relationship. (And of course, worry about safety is only one of seemingly countless other apprehensions.)

Social Anxiety

Social anxiety causes worry, nervousness, and often extreme discomfort in situations that involve interacting with other people. If you have social anxiety, you likely worry about being judged or embarrassed. The thought of being scrutinized is horrifying, and a negative evaluation seems like a crisis. People with social anxiety often avoid social situations to such a degree that their relationships with others become so restricted that they find themselves isolated and lonely.

Common situations that aggravate social anxiety include, but aren't limited to, casual or formal conversations, meeting new people, public speaking, performing, talking on the phone, being in groups, being one-on-one with someone, being assertive, disagreeing or expressing a different opinion, walking into a crowded room, or sitting where people can see you.

Phobias

Phobias are fears about one or more specific situations or objects. They are intense and can be debilitating. When someone encounters that which they fear, their reaction is instant. The fight-or-flight response kicks in, and flight usually wins; alternatively, a freeze reaction can occur, nearly paralyzing the person with fear.

Phobias are irrational fears. Being afraid of water after a near-drowning experience isn't a phobia, but having a life-limiting and misery-causing anxiety about water without a known cause is. (It's officially called aquaphobia and is just one of a seemingly endless list of things that cause distressing fear.) People with phobias know that their fear is irrational, but the reaction is so strong that it takes over rational thoughts and behavior.

Panic Attacks

Panic attacks are short-lived, severe anxiety strikes. They can be part of a condition called panic disorder, a specific type of anxiety disorder that involves excessive worry about having panic attacks in public. Panic attacks can also happen as part of any type of anxiety when a thought or experience triggers an acute reaction. When they do, they're often called anxiety attacks.

Panic (or anxiety) attacks are intense physical reactions that grip people painfully. Panic attacks sweep through the mind and body, causing a sense of impending doom, fear of dying, difficulty breathing, chest pain, nausea, blurred vision, shaking, and dizziness. They often send people to the emergency department of their local hospital because their chest pains mimic a heart attack. Contrary to how they feel, panic attacks aren't fatal, and you can loosen their hold on you.

Worry

Worry can be all-consuming. It can stop you in your tracks and waste an inordinate amount of time. I used to spend a ridiculous amount of time trying to buy a simple greeting card because I'd stand there reading the cards, overanalyzing each one, and worrying about how my recipient would feel about the card and about me for sending it. Worries can be tons of little nuisances like this one that snowball and suffocate you. They can also be about big, heavy topics such as health, death, financial loss, natural disasters, and more. If something exists, someone with anxiety can worry about it. If something doesn't exist but can be imagined, someone with anxiety can worry about it.

Worry is thought-based and involves what-ifs, worst-case scenarios, and automatic negative thoughts—instant, unfavorable assumptions that we make without pausing to think about how true or accurate they are. What we think about grows, so our worries can quickly take us over, spilling into our emotions and actions. In later chapters, we'll be looking more deeply into worrying thoughts. For now, know that you don't have to be plagued with worry forever. You're going to be developing mindfulness, which is an outstanding tool for pulling you out of the worries in your head and putting you into your real life.

Self-Assessment: The Anxiety Checklist

Here, you get to check in with yourself about your own unique anxiety. When you know precisely how your anxiety is limiting your life, you can determine what you want to change.

Each of the statements below relates to anxiety. Check all that apply to you and write in others you think of. Then you can look for patterns: Is your anxiety mostly generalized? Social? Do your worries have themes?

This is your own private book, and it's for your benefit rather than anyone's judgment.

- ☐ I worry a lot about many different things.
- ☐ I have a hard time controlling my fear or worry.
- ☐ "Worried sick" applies to me because I often feel physically ill when I'm upset.
- ☐ My anxiety often skyrockets when I'm stressed.
- ☐ My worries stick with me.
- ☐ I often feel alone because I avoid people.
- ☐ If I have a problem, it's easier to worry about it than ask for help.
- ☐ I miss work or school when my anxiety keeps me locked at home.
- ☐ Sometimes, I feel like I'm going crazy and need to escape.
- ☐ The world is a scary place where a lot of bad things can happen.
- ☐ I have one or more phobias that prevent me from doing things I'd like to do.

_____

_____

_____

I invite you to reflect more deeply in your notebook by building on this checklist. Consider the impact anxiety has on your sense of who you are and how you're living your life. The more honest and open you are with yourself, the more specific you can be as you work through this book. An important tip: Reflect without judging yourself harshly! This is difficult to do with anxiety, so approach this like a neutral observer. You already know you dislike anxiety, and you constantly hear anxiety's negative labels. This isn't about fueling these thoughts and feelings but instead is a chance for you to think objectively about how anxiety is limiting your life so you can do something about it.

It Can Be Better

If thinking about your anxiety on a deeper level than you might be used to is bringing up uncomfortable feelings, that's okay. It's normal and to be expected. Overcoming big life challenges is overwhelming.

Maybe you've tried to beat anxiety before but have faced obstacles. Change, even positive change, is difficult. All living things, including humans, are hardwired for homeostasis, which simply means we're driven to keep things as they are because it's often safer and easier than any change. Homeostasis is a natural resistance to change, even positive change like reducing anxiety. Also, anxiety is a master at its own homeostasis. It has all sorts of tools to use against you when you try to move past it (more on its tricks in later chapters). You might even share this common worry: Why am I spending time helping myself instead of spending time on things I "should" be doing? How dare I be that selfish?

These are universal reasons why people often give up on their quest for a life without anxiety. You probably have other personal reasons, too. Acknowledge these as legitimate, and then put them aside. Here are just a few reasons why you've got this:

- Dedication, attitude, patience, and action are stronger than anxiety's resistance. Change happens and is as natural as homeostasis. You've chosen change, and that's what you'll make happen.
- Negative, anxious thoughts seem real, but just because you think something doesn't make it true. The human brain has plasticity, which means it's malleable and can learn. You have the mental and biological capability to replace your anxious thoughts with positive, realistic ones.

- Motivation and action lead to positive change regardless of how big is the obstacle in front of you or how many times you think you've failed. You've already come this far on your journey. Keep wanting freedom from anxiety and do more of what works for you. You will succeed.
- Your journey is neither a competition nor a race. You can take the information in this book and make it yours, creating personal meaning in it and living it in your own way at your own pace. You no longer have to worry about how you're measuring up to others. That freedom will help you fly.
- Life is lived in the present. This is a new moment in your journey toward calm well-being. You can work through your anxiety, shape your perspective, and improve your life! It happens mindfully in each moment.

Why Mindfulness for Anxiety?

Alleviating anxiety through mindfulness isn't a cute, trendy fad that will fade when the next newfangled method pops onto the scene. Far from it. Mindfulness is perhaps the oldest, most well-established approach to well-being in human history. It has deep roots, thousands of years old, in both religious and secular cultures across the world. From what historians can gather, mindfulness was practiced more than 4,000 years ago in the area of the world we now call Pakistan. It has been an integral part of Hinduism since its inception as far back as 2,500 years ago in what is now India. Mindfulness is also strongly tied to Buddhism, which began around 500 BCE in what is now India and Nepal and spread throughout parts of Asia. Judaism, Christianity, and Islam also incorporate mindfulness into their traditions. Mindfulness isn't exclusively religious, however, as it stands independently from religious belief and practice. It persists because it works to help people create a high-quality life and live it well.

Our current culture demands evidence beyond tradition and stories, and modern science has been on a mission to test mindfulness's ability to reduce anxiety. The results have been largely positive. A 2010 study in the American Psychological Association's journal *Emotion* examined a program called mindfulness-based stress reduction (MBSR), founded by prominent mindfulness expert Jon Kabat-Zinn. The study found that when people practiced mindfulness and breath-focused attention, they decreased anxiety and emotional reactivity to stress and increased self-esteem, emotional regulation, and a sense of calm. Another 2010 study conducted by researchers from Weill Cornell Medicine Medical College and the JFK Medical Center Neuroscience Institute found that MBSR enhances cognitive behavioral therapy (CBT), and when people with generalized anxiety disorder (GAD) practiced mindfulness-based cognitive therapy (MBCT), their anxiety and mood symptoms decreased significantly compared to using CBT alone.

Perhaps even more encouraging than those studies is research that emerged from a 2010 UCLA study. Researchers looked at trait mindfulness and found that people with this characteristic responded less emotionally and negatively to stressors and experienced low amounts of anxiety. Trait mindfulness is a natural tendency to pay attention to the present moment and remain open, accepting, and nonjudgmental in any situation—qualities that are associated with reduced anxiety and enhanced by mindfulness. The wonderful thing about this is that trait mindfulness, while inherent in some people, can be learned and lived. Even if you have been prone to anxiety your entire life or have been told that you had an "anxious personality" (I was told that long ago and have since transcended that artificial designation), you can learn mindfulness and internalize it as a character trait, way of being, and approach to living.

What Is Mindfulness?

Although they are closely related, mindfulness and meditation are not the same thing. Like meditation, mindfulness involves quieting and focusing the mind in any given moment. There is also a type of meditation called mindfulness meditation, in which thoughts are focused on a sensation in the present moment instead of on a mantra, the breath, or something else. However, mindfulness stands on its own and doesn't have to be done seated on a meditation cushion. It goes where you go and is active with you. It's always part of you and can keep you free from anxiety.

Being mindful is nothing more and nothing less than showing up for the present moment of your life. When you are mindful, your mind is full of the tangible stuff around you, the things that can be taken in with your senses and felt with all of your being. When you are mindful, you experience yourself and your life at face value, without expectations, judgments, analyses, or subjective interpretation. In other words, you experience and accept your world as it is, without worrying about how things should be, what something might mean, or which bad things might happen.

Mindfulness is within you. It's a state of being, a mind-set, that helps you flow through life unencumbered by anxiety. Mindfulness involves skills that you can develop and hone, such as observation, acceptance, awareness, and openness to what is. When you have these skills, you won't be stuck in fear and worry, hypervigilant for problems and things that might go wrong. When you're living fully in your present moment, you won't be caught up in ruminations about the past or freak-outs about the future. You can move freely with the ebb and flow, ups and downs, of life and position yourself to respond rationally rather than react anxiously.

Mindfulness is simple—but deceptively so. It's a way of being, and it's also a skill. Because the brain is accustomed to trying to solve problems, it doesn't let go easily. That's why you'll be developing and working on mindfulness skills throughout this book. It takes practice, patience, and trust that mindful living brings inner peace and calm despite stress, challenges, and, yes, anxieties that pop into the mind. If you don't trust mindfulness yet, I invite you to trust me. It took a while for mindfulness to come naturally to me, and I'm so glad I gave it a shot and persevered. I discovered that I have more patience and persistence than anxiety does! My reward is a true sense of contentment with myself and my life. Trust me, and trust yourself.

The (Many) Benefits of Mindfulness

As you work through your anxiety and disengage from it by practicing mindfulness, you will reap other benefits for yourself and your life. Mindfulness is a way of being that invites a state of well-being. These are some of the benefits mindfulness can offer:

A balanced and positive perspective. Mindfulness shifts your perspective from what is wrong to what is right. It allows you to keep a positive perspective in the face of adversity while still being able to acknowledge problems and deal with them well.

Self-acceptance. You may recall that a 2010 study found that mindfulness increases self-esteem. Mindfulness connects you with yourself, your true self. As you worry less about others and situations, and shift your negative, critical thoughts, you discover who you really are.

Better physical health. Mindfulness activities like slow, deep breathing and mindful eating can directly and positively impact health. Your blood becomes oxygen-rich and bathes your brain and body, your heart rate slows, and your blood pressure lowers. Mindful eating often leads to healthier eating. And as you reduce your anxiety, your brain no longer floods your body with stress hormones.

Help overcome depression. Mindful living can have a profound impact on depression. Like anxiety, depression involves ruminating. Repeatedly thinking about problems, one's faults, and other negative subjects both contributes to depression and keeps people stuck in it. Mindfulness can be effective in helping people overcome depression by grounding them in the present moment and helping them attend to the positive. This increases motivation and energy, and leads to more positive change.

A medication-free approach. Mindfulness comes from within. It's an attitude, mentality, action, and skill. It is an approach to anxiety that has no harsh side effects and is cost-free.

What Mindfulness Is Not

Because "mindfulness" is a popular term, there are many opinions and misconceptions about it. Sadly, misunderstandings can lead people to dismiss mindfulness and miss a way of being that reduces anxiety, helps counter depression, enhances well-being, and opens them to life. Let's put to rest some common misconceptions about mindfulness.

Mindfulness is not:

Religious. People commonly mistake mindfulness for religion. Mindfulness isn't a religion, and you don't have to belong to a certain religion to use it. Some religious traditions do incorporate mindfulness and meditation, especially in prayer. Mindfulness can have a spiritual component if you choose to integrate your beliefs into your mindful way of being, but it can also be completely secular. Mindfulness is a highly personal experience that by itself doesn't have a religious or spiritual component.

A quick fix. Mindfulness is a way of being with yourself that develops over time. It's a gradual process of learning to live firmly rooted in the present moment. Be patient and forgiving with yourself as you embrace mindfulness, and celebrate little victories, moments when you remained present and enjoyed your family, a friend, or a walk in nature. Mindful experiences build on one another until they come regularly and naturally.

A cure-all. I promise you that I am not a charlatan selling snake oil to cure you of all that ails you. Mindfulness doesn't directly cure anything, including anxiety. Instead, it replaces anxious thoughts, feelings, and behaviors with effective ones that ultimately override anxiety. Mindfulness can't stop problems from invading your life, nor can it magically fix a bad relationship or find you a job. What mindfulness does is empower you with the skills and perspective to make things happen for yourself.

Time-constrained. Mindfulness isn't a one-and-done tool. It doesn't expire. Mindfulness is timeless because it's part of who you are. You aren't doomed to failure if you don't "get it" in a certain amount of time. It's a lifelong process to be embraced and enjoyed on your time. You might be thinking, "But this book is time-constrained because it's an eight-week plan." Don't fret! It's simply organized that way to provide useful structure. Your journey will continue after the last page, and you'll be ready to forge ahead!

Something outside yourself. Mindfulness works so well for anxiety because it comes from within you. With mindfulness, the calm you create doesn't come from a gadget you fiddle with or external rules you follow. As you recognize and embrace the power that lives fully inside of you, you will break free from anxiety, your self-confidence will grow, and your anxiety will shrink even more. Mindfulness is a perspective, mind-set, choice, and approach to life that is completely within you and already part of who you are. Imagine what it will be like to develop it!

Only for those who already have inner peace. It can seem like inner peace is a trait that people either have or don't have. It can also appear that mindfulness happens once people are at peace and live without anxiety. If you've ever wished that you could be mindful and peaceful but can't because anxiety is in your way, take heart. It's the other way around. Mindfulness comes first, and inner peace is the result. Peace must be developed and honed, and mindfulness is one of the most powerful ways to do it.

Always easy. The concept of mindfulness is deceptively simple. The practice, however, takes time to learn. If you have struggled with anxiety, are trapped in its negative thoughts and emotions, and are restricted in what you do, it will take work to break the patterns. If anxiety were easy to get rid of, no one would live with it. We could just brush it aside, unbothered. As you and I well know, anxiety isn't easy to shake. (Also, remember homeostasis, the process within all living things that makes change difficult.) Mindfulness replaces anxiousness, but it's not always easy to do. Be kind to yourself and be persistent. The easy way isn't usually the best, most lasting way to accomplish anything, including learning mindfulness and reducing anxiety.

Complementary Treatment

Mindfulness is one of the most effective, medication-free methods to help treat anxiety, but it isn't the only one. Other approaches for reducing anxiety are effective, too. Many are part of mental health therapy, and people learn these techniques or tools while working with a counselor or other professional. Mindfulness is often integrated into other strategies to give people a broad repertoire of tools to work with. Remember the study conducted by researchers at Weill Cornell Medicine Medical College and the JFK Medical Center Neuroscience Institute? It found that combining mindfulness with cognitive behavioral therapy was more successful in helping people lower anxiety than CBT alone. Being open to different healing approaches will help you create the most effective personal plan to rid yourself of anxiety.

A few approaches proven to be successful in reducing anxiety include:

Cognitive behavioral therapy (CBT). CBT helps people identify the automatic negative thoughts that contribute to anxiety. When people are aware of their unhelpful thinking patterns, they can change them in ways that positively affect what they do and how they live.

Acceptance and commitment therapy (ACT). ACT is a powerful healing approach that uses mindfulness as one of its primary components. ACT helps people learn to accept what can't be changed, such as the past, and teaches strategies on how to separate themselves from problems. Mindfulness, self-observation, and awareness allow people to develop personal insights into their thoughts, emotions, and behaviors that may be contributing to anxiety. Then identifying and embracing values and committing to act on them help people live an authentic, quality, anxiety-free life.

Biofeedback. This is a procedure that helps you recognize your body's physical responses to anxiety and learn to control them. Using electrodes or sensors attached painlessly to your skin, biofeedback increases your awareness of involuntary anxiety reactions like increased heart rate and blood pressure, flushed skin, and other physiological reactions to stress and anxiety. Once your awareness is heightened, you can learn to control anxiety reactions with techniques like deep breathing, progressive muscle relaxation, guided imagery—and, yes, mindfulness.

Hypnosis. When someone participates in hypnotherapy, they are placed into a trancelike state in order to promote deep relaxation. The idea is to allow the conscious mind, the thinking mind that is agitated and anxious, to rest, and the subconscious mind to emerge and process anxiety. This helps the therapist create a tailored plan for the client to reduce anxiety.

Anxiety is stubborn. It often takes a combination of approaches, different for each individual, to treat it. In this book, you'll learn how to use mindfulness, a powerful way to become untangled and anxiety-free.

Takeaways

Congratulations! You have completed the first step in your journey to freedom. You have begun to unravel anxiety by deepening your understanding of what it is and how it interferes in your life. You've learned about mindfulness, so you have a solid foundation upon which to build as you learn how to use it to help anxiety.

Let these key points carry you forward into week one of your eight-week plan:

- Anxiety is a real experience. You're not making it up or overreacting.
- It's all-encompassing, affecting your brain and body, thoughts, emotions, and behavior.
- You might experience anxiety, fear, or both. Anxiety is past- or future-oriented, while fear is usually present-focused.
- The experience of anxiety is slightly different for everyone. All anxiety involves worry, and it takes different forms like generalized anxiety, social anxiety, phobias, and panic attacks.
- Mindfulness is both a time-honored and research-proven approach to reducing anxiety.
- Mindfulness is a mind-set within you, a way of being with yourself and the world that involves paying attention to the present moment with openness, awareness, and acceptance.

*Anxiety happens when
you think you have to figure out
everything all at once.
Breathe.
You're strong.
You got this.
Take it day by day.*

—Karen Salmansohn

CHAPTER TWO

WEEK ONE:

Getting Familiar with Your Anxiety

Welcome to your first week of action to untangle your anxiety and empower yourself to live unencumbered by negative thoughts and feelings! This week, you'll begin to develop deeper insights into just how much our thoughts nurture our anxiety. You'll get to know some of your personal anxiety triggers so that you have a clearer idea of the core issues that are bogging you down. You'll empower yourself by setting some of your own treatment goals, too. You'll also engage in mindfulness exercises to help you live outside of your head, away from worries and fears, and fully and peacefully in your present moment. Let's take this day by day and walk together along your path to freedom!

How Thoughts Lead to Anxiety

Before beginning in earnest, I want to ease any anxiety you might have that something is "wrong" with you or that your anxiety troubles are your own fault because you're thinking negative thoughts. Neither of those is true at all.

The human mind has focused on problems for nearly 300,000 years because, in our earliest days, we had to think constantly about threats and danger. After such extensive training, the brain still today automatically defaults to negative thoughts and interpretations of situations to keep us alert and safe. This is true of everyone's brain, even the calmest of mindfulness gurus. It's not just you. Because of automatically generated negative thoughts, everyone experiences some anxiety from time to time. Some people have discovered how to distance themselves from these negative, anxious thoughts and enjoy inner peace and calm, while tens of millions of others are stuck in anxiety-provoking thoughts. With 40 million sufferers in the United States alone, anxiety disorders are the most common of all mental illnesses. The National Institute of Mental Health reports that in any 12-month period, about 20 percent of Americans live with an anxiety disorder and that almost one-third experience an anxiety disorder at some point in their lifetime.

While anxiety is a common problem, the way anxiety is experienced is unique to each of us. You learned a bit about specific types of anxiety disorders in the last chapter. Here's a look at what they can be like for someone living with them. Let's take an ordinary situation like a third-grade parent-teacher conference and see how anxiety turns it into a nightmare for Nate, a father who suffers from extreme anxiety with multiple components.

Do you recognize your own thought patterns in any of these situations?

Generalized Anxiety

As Nate paced the hallway outside the closed classroom door, waiting to be summoned by the teacher, his mind raced with what-ifs and worst-case scenarios. What if his son was still behind in his reading ability? What if he had a learning disorder? Did the teacher want to put him in special education? Would that help or hurt him? What if it made kids tease him? Aren't kids who are bullied at risk of dropping out of school? And if he's already behind academically, he wouldn't have the skills he'd need to support himself in life. He'd probably turn into one of those single, lonely, bitter men who still lives in his parents' basement playing video games day and night. Video games! Nate was the one who insisted on getting their son the big gaming system for his birthday.

This is all his fault. He should be giving his son books and science kits, not video games. And he should spend more time with him instead of working so much. But if he didn't work so much, how could they afford to keep their house? He'd considered talking to his boss about a schedule change before, but he never did because he knew his boss would fire him on the spot. He just couldn't lose that job, especially now that his son might have a learning disability. Don't disabilities like that require a lot of special resources, resources that are expensive? He might need to find a second job, but just the one job already made him a terrible father by keeping him away from his son too much. This was a disaster. His poor little boy was doomed, and Nate was powerless to do anything about it.

Before the teacher even invited him into the classroom, Nate's anxious thoughts had fed off each other and spiraled out of control. A closer look at Nate would reveal that he was sweating and trembling and afraid that he would vomit. He endured the conference with extreme discomfort and, in the car on the way home, he was shocked that his wife was cheerful and happy about the meeting. Nate realized that he didn't know what the teacher had said because he was too caught up in his thoughts and imagined scenarios.

Social Anxiety

Nate thought his anxiety about his son's future filled his whole being, but to his dismay, the moment the teacher opened the door and beckoned him inside, new anxiety elbowed its way into his mind. How could he hide his inadequacy from this teacher? He couldn't. Her judgmental eyes bore into his, and there was something aggressive and mocking in her handshake. He knew that his sweaty palms disgusted her. Her greeting was short and terse. She had clearly already found him to be the worst of all parents she had ever met. Well, she now knew the answer to why his son had problems. Nate wasn't good enough to help his son learn. Nate wasn't good enough to prevent the bullying. What was this teacher writing down? Probably notes for his son's file, to warn other teachers and other schools about Nate's horrible parenting. His gut twisted painfully, and his temples throbbed in reaction to the truth.

Nate's social anxiety is most intense when he is around someone he perceives to be an authority figure, like his son's teacher. Social anxiety can be limited to certain situations or people, or it can rear its ugly head wherever you go and whenever you are around other people. Social anxiety disorder, also called social phobia because it is an intense, specific fear, bothers people in different ways. Nate can force himself into social situations but endures them with severe discomfort. Other people have such high anxiety about being judged or embarrassing themselves that they completely avoid people and places and remain isolated at home.

There's good news about social anxiety. Like other forms of anxiety, it involves thoughts. Thoughts aren't real, despite how they may feel. Thoughts are a bit like clay in that they can be worked and shaped, held in your hand, or dropped and kicked across the street.

Phobias

Nate's phobia is social phobia. Other phobias behave similarly and can involve almost anything. Strong fear of an object or situation penetrates someone's entire being. Sensing a feared object (seeing it, feeling it, hearing it, smelling it, or tasting it) or thinking about a feared object instantaneously activates the sympathetic nervous system. If this happens to you, you are catapulted into instant alert. Your brain releases epinephrine, norepinephrine, and cortisol. Your adrenal glands on your kidneys release adrenaline. Your heart rate increases and the contractions of your heart are stronger (hence the common feeling of cardiac arrest). Blood is diverted from your skin and gut to your skeletal muscles. You are automatically prepared to fight or flee. What often happens instead, however, is that you freeze and feel helpless to do anything at all.

Phobias feel out of control because your body's response is automatic. You do nothing to cause this fear reaction other than sense or think something. Don't be fooled! You most definitely aren't helpless, and you do indeed have control. As you use knowledge and mindfulness to untangle your anxiety, you can even override your sympathetic nervous system.

Panic Attacks

As his wife drove them home, Nate watched her beam with apparent pride for their son. Nate felt ill. Why was she so happy? What had he missed? This was another example of his inadequacy as a dad. He shivered involuntarily. Everything felt wrong. Something horrible was about to happen. Suddenly, all his worries of the night exploded, and his chest tightened. Hot pain tore through his upper body. He couldn't breathe. He'd been through this before, but this time was worse. This time, it was most certainly a heart attack. He heard his wife's voice, but he couldn't make out what she was saying. He couldn't make out her expression because everything was blurry. He felt the car come to a screeching stop, and he opened his door, gasping for air. His wife stuck a paper bag in his face, and he grabbed it and breathed into it. It helped. Within minutes, his breathing and heart rate began to return to normal. He had been wired with nervous energy, but now he was drained and exhausted. Feeling ashamed and inadequate, he sat in silence as his wife drove them home.

When anxious thoughts are intense, they can suddenly erupt into a panic or anxiety attack. They can make you feel like the world and all its problems, along with all your own worries and fears, are descending upon you at warp speed, crushing you and blocking out everything but anxiety, panic, and the fear that you're dying.

While it can seem impossible to escape from the vise of anxiety attacks, it is truly very possible. Breathe easy. You can learn to de-escalate panic attacks while they're happening and prevent them from beginning in the first place.

Worry

Nate experiences several types of anxiety, which is common. Anxiety is formed of many different types of negative thoughts, and while they're sorted out and categorized to make them easier to understand and help, in real life worries can overlap. While you might recognize some of your own types of anxieties in this single snapshot of Nate's experience, the specific nature of your worries and the effects they have on you will be unique. How very thoughtful of anxiety to tailor itself to each person.

To begin to rein in your anxiety, it's helpful to be able to identify and describe what worries are like for you. Start to pay attention to the specific worries you often have. Nate's extreme concerns about his son and the teacher's negative opinion developed so quickly and were so automatic that he believed them and didn't have a chance to mentally step away from them. Therefore, his worries spiraled out of control and tangled him in a knot so tight that he experienced a panic attack. When you increase your awareness of your type(s) of anxiety, the nature of your worries, and your specific thoughts, you can recognize them when they start to happen. You'll then be able to see them not as the truth but as an inaccurate interpretation of what's happening.

Cultivating mindfulness allows you to form a space between you and your thoughts. Nate didn't have this space, and his worries consumed him. Your journey to spacious living begins now.

Mindful Moment

 Every Mindful Moment that you'll encounter in this book is an exercise to help you cultivate your own mindful way of being and living. You might consider keeping a list in your notebook of the exercises you really love and want to use regularly. You can also make note of your own thoughts for modifying the exercises. This is your book, your notebook, your mindful moments, and yourself. Create your mindful life! Ready? Here's your first Mindful Moment.

Pause for pranayama breathing. In the traditions of yoga, *prana* refers to our life force, our breath, and *pranayama* is the intentional practice of controlling that life force. Pranayama helps you be mindful by anchoring yourself in your breath right here, right now. Practice it now:

1. Close your eyes and pay attention to your breathing.
2. Place your hands on your belly.
3. Begin to breathe slowly, deeply, and with control.
4. Inhale deeply while counting very slowly until your lungs are full and your belly and diaphragm have expanded.
5. Pause and hold your breath for about five counts.
6. Gently and slowly exhale, completely emptying your lungs and letting your belly and diaphragm sink and relax.
7. Let your thoughts drift while you listen to the sound of your breath and feel its rhythm.
8. When anxieties pop in, return your attention to your breathing.

Repeat several times. Consider setting a soft timer or chime for about five minutes (more or less according to your preference) and giving in to the rhythm until the timer sounds.

Your Breath, Your (Quality) Life

The core of mindfulness is deep within you: your breath. Simply by choosing to breathe slowly and deeply, and tuning in to the sound and sensation of your breath, you effect many positive changes in your body that allow you to slow down, relax, and be still. Research is showing that controlling your breath this way activates your parasympathetic nervous system, dubbed "rest and digest" (this is the opposite of the sympathetic, or "fight-or-flight," nervous system). This, in turn, slows your heart rate and blood pressure, increases theta waves in your brain (responsible for relaxation, creativity, and flow), and synchronizes neural activity in the heart, lungs, and limbic system (the emotional center of your brain). It just so happens that purposeful deep breathing also positively impacts the cerebral cortex, the outer layer of your brain responsible for such crucial things as intelligence, personality, language, planning, thinking, and sensory processing. Anxiety involves language and thinking, and mindfulness involves tuning into the senses and being fully planted in your present moment. Deep breathing affects the cerebral cortex, where all of this takes place. This is why regularly pausing to breathe well is an important component of mindfulness and a good way to soothe anxiety.

Safety Behaviors

Anxiety is hard to live with and can make seemingly ordinary situations uncomfortable at best and excruciating at worst. Many times, people would rather avoid a situation than endure it, but that's not always possible (or even a good idea). To make it through, people sometimes use "safety behaviors." These are actions taken, usually intentionally but at other times subconsciously, to make a person feel safer and more secure when they can't escape an agonizing situation.

Here are just a few examples of common safety behaviors for anxiety:

- Staying close to an exit so you can easily leave as quickly as possible
- Pretending to be busy on a cell phone or reading a book to keep people at bay
- Carrying comfort objects in your pocket, such as a small stone or a pen that can be clicked
- Constantly checking to ensure that a loved one is okay
- Seeking reassurance that you are behaving/acting right, such as frequently asking someone if they're having a good time with you
- Needing to have someone with you for support
- Wearing hoodies, hats, scarves, or other clothing that "hides" you

Safety behaviors may seem harmless, but they often reinforce anxiety by sending a subtle message that you do have something to fear and that you are incapable of handling yourself without these behaviors. Further, some safety behaviors, like using alcohol or drugs to cope with anxiety, can be dangerous.

Mindfulness is a healthy alternative to safety behaviors because it is a way of centering your attention that calms your mind and body. Mindfulness allows you to take in sights, sounds, smells, and textures to shift your thoughts from worries and fears to what is really going on right where you are, right now.

Anxiety Triggers

Anxiety triggers are anything that causes or increases anxiety. Everyone's anxiety triggers are unique to them. Thoughts of being criticized or judged negatively used to make me very anxious, but you might not be bothered by that at all. Something else entirely might rev up your worries. Knowing what triggers your anxiety is an important part of your labor of self-love to free yourself from anxiety's grip. When you can get specific and determine what, precisely, makes you anxious, you can successfully deal with it by creating your own personal treatment plan.

Consider these major life areas and what affects your anxiety level:

Social Interactions

Social anxiety ranges from shyness to complete avoidance. When you're around others in any setting—perhaps even your own home—your anxiety might be triggered by worries about what you "should" or "shouldn't" say or do. You might find your own triggers by watching for signs of disapproval from friends, families, enemies, and strangers. When your own anxiety is sparked in social settings, you can't listen, laugh, and be relaxed and fully present. Anxiety is a barbed-wire fence—electrified at that—that separates you from those in your life.

Education or Career

Anxiety at school or work can be a glass ceiling that prevents you from succeeding to the degree you want to. Sometimes, your own internal pressures are your worst triggers in these settings. Bullying yourself into needing to be perfect or worrying about what you think of as failing can interfere with your success. In extreme cases, your worries about what might happen to you if you're not good enough can trigger a physical illness that keeps you in bed rather than at your desk. This sparks more worries about new consequences, and anxiety gives itself an "A" or a raise while you suffer.

Health and Well-Being

Regardless of what triggers your anxiety, all worries, and all their triggers, can wreak havoc on your health and well-being. While anxiety is a mental health disorder, it is also a physical health issue. When something triggers your anxiety, it sets off a physiological stress reaction that affects mind, body, and spirit. You can feel anxiety in every system of your body, and feeling anxious and ill can keep you from living your life fully.

Interestingly, did you know that our gut is dubbed our second brain, and we really have three nervous systems rather than two? The enteric nervous system is in and around our gut, and it's in constant communication with the brain. Those butterflies in your stomach are anxious little insects, and when it comes to anxiety triggers, you might not want to automatically listen to your gut instinct.

Everyday Responsibility

Anxiety has a way of preventing you from being who you want to be and living how you want to live. Worries and fears disrupt us in one or more of our life roles. When something triggers your fight-flight-or-freeze response, you are blocked from doing what you need and want to do. When anxiety flares, you might be unable to do all that you need to do as a parent, such as meeting with your child's teacher when your child is experiencing problems. It can prevent you from being the significant other, friend, volunteer, or simply the active person you want to be.

 What triggers your anxiety? Where and when does anxiety show up in your life? What are the circumstances? How does it interfere with what you do and how you feel about yourself? Give yourself time to reflect on your anxiety triggers so you know where to begin untangling the knot.

Set Action Goals

Once you are aware of what causes or worsens your specific anxiety, you can address it. Identifying and facing your triggers arms you with the information you need to create your treatment goals. Here, you have the opportunity to create and shape your goals for a life unencumbered by anxiety. This is an empowering process! Maybe no one has ever really asked you what you want for yourself (or maybe they have but didn't genuinely listen to your response). That's in the past. You're living now. I'm sincerely asking you that question in this moment. But much, much more important than my asking is you asking yourself and listening to your own response.

To help you in this process, I'm going to borrow from a type of treatment known as solution-focused therapy and present you with the Miracle Question: Imagine that while you were sleeping one night, a miracle occurred, and all your anxiety disappeared. When you woke up in the morning, how would you know that this miracle had occurred? What would be different? What would you do differently? What would others notice?

Setting goals is a process of discovering what you do want instead of what you don't. Rather than framing your goals in terms of what you want to change, describe what you will have when you achieve your goal.

 Write your responses to the next three questions in your notebook.

1. When your anxiety is gone, what will you be able to do?

    List or describe at least three things that are important to you, but anxiety prevents you from doing. (Remember, focus on what you'll build, not on what's wrong now.) These are some of your top values, your reasons why you are untangling your anxiety.

2. What will your relationship with yourself be like when anxiety
    is gone?

    Anxiety robs you of your sense of self, including self-confidence
    and self-efficacy (the belief in your ability to succeed in things that
    are important to you). Who are you at your core? How will you handle
    stress? Here, you're solidifying how you'll be when you're free.

3. What action steps do I need to take?

    Action is as important as vision. What little things can you do,
    moment by moment, to achieve your vision and live your values?
    How will you respond differently to your current anxiety triggers?

Be thoughtful as you set your goals, and give yourself permission to
work toward them step by small step. That's how progress is made! Know,
too, that these actions may be difficult at first. After all, if you knew what
to do and how to do it, you'd already be doing them. You'll solidify your
action goals as you move through the book, page by page.

Takeaways

Your first week of extracting yourself from anxiety has been productive! You've learned more about your own anxiety and what it's doing to you. Getting specific helps you know what you want and how to achieve it. You have also begun mindful living with two exercises (there's one right after this) to use when you're trapped in anxious thoughts. Here's a recap of what you've discovered in this chapter:

- Anxiety is incredibly common, affecting everyone in some way.
- Much of our anxiety originates in and is perpetuated by our thoughts.
- Our anxious thoughts have triggers that set them in motion. Identifying your triggers can help you change your response to them.
- When you develop your treatment goals and think in terms of what you want when your anxiety is gone, you empower yourself to take action steps away from anxiety.

Mindful Moment—Go with the Grain (of Rice)

In this moment of mindfulness, you'll use your sense of touch to pull yourself out of your anxious thoughts and into your tangible world.

Gather a large container or gallon-size storage bag and some raw rice (you can use sand or Epsom salts instead). Fill your container about half full of rice. Set a timer for five minutes. Settle into a comfortable seat and plunge your hands into the container. Feel the rice surround your hand and fill the spaces between your fingers. Lift your hands gently and notice the sensation of the rice cascading through those spaces. Squeeze your hands into fists around the grains of rice. Continue to play gently, fully noticing what your hands are experiencing. When your mind wanders and you notice thoughts, anxious or otherwise, simply return to your rice play until the timer sounds.

 Brainstorm! How will you use the sense of touch to pull yourself away from anxious thoughts and into the moment when you don't have your bag of rice?

*Negative thoughts stick
around because we believe them,
not because we want them
or choose them.*

—**Andrew Bernstein**

CHAPTER THREE

WEEK TWO:
Negative Thoughts

Thoughts are nothing more than insubstantial chemical activity in an organ we call the brain. On their own, they're nothing. The life-invading problem with negative thoughts begins because they're sticky. We attach to them and get stuck. Like a glob of putty stuck in a linty pocket, negative thoughts attract gunk (other similar thoughts) and grow into a disgusting lump of doubt and distrust (in ourselves, in the world, and in situations) that clings to you, overtaking other thoughts and trapping us in an anxious state of existence. In this chapter, we'll explore negative thoughts and learn how to neutrally observe them rather than wrestling with them and getting more deeply engulfed in their goo. You'll use mindfulness to create welcome space between you and your thoughts so you have room to live.

The Negative Thought Cycle

The famous philosopher René Descartes boldly declared, "*Cogito, ergo sum*." *I think, therefore I am*. We might expand that: *I think, therefore I am anxious*. While anxiety is too complex to have a single, simple cause, it is true that our thoughts are a significant source of our anxiety. More specifically, the nature of our thoughts and the degree to which we believe them are forces underlying our worries and fears.

From the moment we are born, we take in the world around us, first through our senses and rudimentary emotions, later with words. We assign meaning to all that we take in. Are we safe? Loved? Do we have some freedom and control over our lives? When basic needs like this are unmet—even the slightest bit—we become stressed, anxious, and problem-oriented and our thoughts become increasingly negative. In cognitive behavioral therapy, they're called automatic negative thoughts, or ANTs. We interpret our world through negative thought patterns, and we become stuck in anxiety as a result. There are numerous types of ANTs. Just a few that are active in anxiety include:

Black-and-white thinking, or all-or-nothing thinking. When we have anxiety, we think in extremes. A problem isn't situational and temporary but instead is a disaster that will ruin a good portion of our lives. "I blew this presentation, and now I won't get that promotion."

Catastrophizing or magnification. When we catastrophize, we blow a problem way out of proportion. After a tiff with your teenage daughter, you might think, "I'm the worst parent in the world. No wonder my daughter hates me. We'll never have a good relationship, and it's all my fault for always screwing up with her."

Overgeneralizing. This type of thinking involves applying one outcome to many different situations. Using words like "always," "never," "everything," or "nothing" signals that you may be overgeneralizing. If you're at lunch with a group of people and inadvertently put your foot in your mouth, you might feel instantly mortified and think, "I always say such stupid things and ruin everything! No wonder people never ask me to do things with them."

Jumping to conclusions, or mind reading. Anxiety causes us to watch for problems and make all sorts of negative assumptions. You just know that your wife is unhappy because of you or that phone call from the same unknown number is someone trying to reach you about a credit problem.

Our automatic negative thoughts feed off each other and run away with our imagination, making us increasingly stressed, anxious, and miserable. The way out is by returning to the way we initially took in the world around us and even learned about ourselves: with our senses. That's right. We were born mindful. Now all we need to do is home in on the peaceful state of being.

Sit with Your Thoughts

Anxiety's negative thoughts come automatically, without us thinking them on purpose. They become a problem when we engage with them. Whether we believe them and let them affect our other thoughts, feelings, and actions, or disagree with them and argue, we are tangling with them. We become stuck because our focus is on our black-and-white, overgeneralized thoughts that make us jump to anxiety-provoking conclusions.

Instead of ruminating about them, try simply sitting with them in open awareness. Thich Nhat Hanh, a Buddhist monk and mindfulness guru, speaks of shining your awareness on your thoughts like warm sunshine. Instead of judging your thoughts—and yourself—simply observe them and let them come and go naturally while you go about your real life. The process looks something like this:

- **When you find yourself anxious, pause and breathe slowly and deeply.**
- **Tune in to the thoughts racing through your mind, but don't try to catch them. Just notice them.**
- **Visualize warm sunlight filling you and radiating through your being, illuminating your anxious thoughts.**
- **Enjoy the warm sun, and just watch your thoughts run around without joining them, expanding on them, or judging them in any way.**
- **When you just watch, you'll notice that they have nothing to stick to, so they slip away without bothering you.**

This works because thoughts aren't tangible things. They're also largely inaccurate. They pop into the mind uninvited and act as if they're hard-and-fast truths. The real truth, though, is that they're unreliable and unreal. If you are fretting over a conflict you had with your partner earlier in the day, it's not an actual event happening now. Your partner isn't present with you in this thought. Your memory of the things that were said and body language you picked up is skewed by your anxious emotions. Actively thinking about this situation keeps it happening in your mind—but only in the way your anxious thoughts make it play out. In the meantime, your real moment is happening without you being fully in it.

> *How freeing it is to know that*
>
> *if we do not attend to a thought, answer it,*
>
> *change it, identify with it, and all the rest,*
>
> *it literally ceases to exist. If we let a thought be*
>
> *nothing, then that's what it will be . . . nothing.*
>
> —**Nancy Colier**, LCSW, author and therapist

I Am Not My Thoughts

Because the brain is programmed to look for problems and try to solve them by fighting, fleeing, or freezing, and because accompanying anxious thoughts come automatically, learning to merely observe your thoughts and shine your light on them without joining them takes time and practice. Use these exercises this week and beyond to help you see that you are not your thoughts.

 You might find it helpful to record your thoughts, impressions, and notes to yourself.

Just a Thought

Horror movies are so terrifying because they stick with us. Thanks to the terrible ideas we're exposed to, coupled with exaggeration and special effects, scenes replay in our mind long after the final credits roll. They seem so real that little things that go bump in the night, like ice cubes dropping into the bin in the freezer, startle us and send our imagination right back into the movie. However, that noise that took your mind back to the horror was really just an ice cube.

The same principle is at work in anxiety. Our anxious thoughts pop into our mind at the slightest "drop of ice," and we magnify them with imagined words, scenarios, and what-ifs. Our reality is usurped by a set of anxious thoughts that seems real but is no more substantial than the last movie you saw.

When you notice yourself immersed in the anxious movie playing in your mind, gently walk out of the theater. Shift your attention to what's happening around you rather than in your mind. Fully notice your real world. Use your sense of touch to ground you in it. Remind yourself that your anxious thoughts are only imaginary things, not real life happening now.

Thought Power

Thoughts are only thoughts, but when we believe them, they have power over us. Reclaim control over your own mind and life by reducing the power your thoughts have over you.

When you sit with your thoughts, notice patterns. Do you worry a lot about loved ones? Do you berate yourself for mistakes and worry about their effects? Chances are, your negative thoughts follow many patterns. Start by identifying one that is particularly troublesome, and gradually chip away at its power over you by creating an affirmation—a simple, positive, reality-based statement that puts your anxiety in perspective. Then keep this statement with you and read it frequently, especially when your powerful anxiety overwhelms you. Here's something I've used:

My anxious thought: "I'm doing this [insert whatever I'm doing at the moment] wrong, and I'll fail."

My affirmation: "I don't need to be perfect to be successful. I do things well, and I keep growing."

Then put mindfulness to work for you by focusing on something right where you are that reinforces your affirmation. I might look at this book or pause when I'm with my family and take in the positive moment.

Counteract a Thought

Cognitive behavioral therapy teaches us to find evidence to counterbalance anxious thoughts. Mindfulness takes it a step further by encouraging us to pay more attention to this evidence in the real world and less attention to thoughts about something that has already happened or hasn't yet occurred.

For example, do you worry that you're an inadequate parent? Shift your focus from imagined shortcomings and back into your real life. Identify positive aspects of your relationship with your children and look for evidence of all you do well as their parent. Perhaps carry with you a reminder of your positive connection to use as a mindfulness object. When you catch yourself worrying about your parenting, hold the object, feel it, and study it to remind yourself of your strengths as a parent.

Thought Evaluation

When we get caught up in our anxious thoughts, either believing them or struggling against them, we miss out on better things, such as enjoying friends and loved ones, hobbies, and, yes, even work or school.

A quick way to shrink an anxious thought is to ask yourself:

- **Is this thought doing anything for me right now?**
- **Is my thought helpful?**
- **Is it truthful beyond any doubt?**
- **Is it important in this moment?**

If the answer is "no," shift your attention to something that is helpful, truthful, or important right now.

Thought Detachment

Sitting with your thoughts and simply observing them neutrally allows you to separate yourself from them. Especially when you know they're not real, helpful, true, or important, you can let them float away from you.

You already know that trying to force your anxiety away doesn't help; it only makes it stickier. Instead, don't grab on to it. Imagine that an anxious thought is on a cloud, drifting away from you on a gentle breeze. Or imagine it as a stick or a leaf floating away on a stream. Harness the power of visualization to picture your thoughts physically moving away from you. The distance you create gives you room to fill with realistic, helpful, non-anxious thoughts.

Worry Time

Sometimes, reducing anxiety temporarily causes new anxiety—the concern that if you don't worry and think about problems, the problems will win. You'll find that isn't true, but it is a legitimate concern when you first start letting go of anxiety. An effective way to help yourself with this new worry is by setting aside dedicated worry time every day.

Devote 10 to 15 minutes every day to worry. Set a timer so you stay within your limit.

Make it the same time every day, such as before or after dinner. (I suggest avoiding making early morning your worry time so you don't start your day on a negative note.)

When a worry pops up during the day, write it down for later, and tell your anxiety to stop. Gently acknowledge your worry and remind yourself that you can return to it. This can reduce the stress associated with temporarily releasing the worry because you know that you will return to it later.

During your worry time, give your anxious thoughts a chance to show up. Often, because you're mindful in this moment and not distracted by other tasks, this turns into a problem-solving time.

When the timer sounds, thank yourself for tending to your concerns and then shift your attention to your present moment.

Monkey Mind

The human brain is a thinking brain. This can be a problem for us when it turns into an overthinking, worrying brain. "Monkey mind" is a Buddhist term that captures the mind's restlessness and how it's easily distracted, jumping and swinging from one thought to another and another and another. Much like a monkey, the mind can be loud, screeching above everything else to be heard. You are not a monkey, and your entire brain is not a monkey brain. You have the power and ability to tame your monkey mind. Mindfulness is a key component. When you notice your monkey mind in action, take several deep breaths and simply tune in to the sound and feel of those breaths. Gently turn your attention to what is happening in your moment rather than in your monkey mind. With patience and practice, you can develop the skill of turning away from the raging monkey and attending to yourself and your life.

Takeaways

You have discovered some important truths about negative, anxious thoughts this week:

- Negative thoughts come automatically, without us trying to create them.
- These thoughts keep us stuck in anxiety rather than living freely and fully in our real world.
- Anxious thoughts follow predictable patterns, such as black-and-white thinking, overgeneralizing, and jumping to conclusions. When we're aware of these, we can recognize them as unreliable products of anxiety rather than as absolute truths.
- Struggling with anxious thoughts only reinforces them because that's what you're paying attention to.
- When you simply sit with your thoughts without engaging with them, observing them and letting them go, you give yourself a chance to mindfully pay attention to your real world.
- By intentionally practicing thought exercises regularly, you decrease anxiety's power and increase your own power in your life.

Mindful Moment—Sit Still, and Sip Your Tea

Just as you sit with your anxious thoughts, you can sit mindfully with positive experiences. The more you learn to sit and be present with what you're doing, the richer your life experiences will become.

Try this now: Brew a cup of hot tea (or coffee or hot chocolate). Settle into a comfortable chair and notice how it feels. Wrap your hands around the mug and feel the warmth seep into your fingers and hands. Visualize the warmth traveling through your body. Raise the mug to your nose and inhale slowly, observing but not evaluating it. Bring the cup to your lips, and sip. Savor the taste and the feel of the heat in your mouth. Pay attention to how it feels as you swallow. Repeat this process as you enjoy your beverage. When anxiety creeps in, just return to the moment.

*In the beginner's mind
there are many possibilities,
but in the expert's,
there are few.*

—Shunryu Suzuki

CHAPTER FOUR

WEEK THREE:
Overcoming Fear of the Unknown

Would you rather settle for a dull night at home or have a friend surprise you with an evening out—but you won't know where you're going or what is involved until you get there? If you opted for the first choice, how does the thought of that unknown evening make you feel, emotionally and physically? What does it make you want to do (or not do)?

If you live with anxiety, chances are high that you aren't a fan of uncertainty. You might even hate or be afraid of the unknown. The mere thought of not knowing what to expect might cause your anxiety to skyrocket.

If you hate the unknown, this chapter is going to help you grow through it. Don't worry about what lies ahead. Simply know that you'll be learning about uncertainty, both intolerance of it and how to accept it. Then a few practical exercises and a mindful moment will gently lead you to freedom from uncertainty anxiety.

Uncertainty Intolerance

For someone with anxiety, not knowing what might happen in a given situation can be miserable. "Uncertainty" comes to mean "disastrous possibilities," and anxiety skyrockets. A 2007 study examining how people handle the unknown found a strong relationship between uncertainty intolerance and anxiety. Researchers observed that while having difficulties with uncertainty isn't the only cause of anxiety, the more uncomfortable people are with ambiguity, the more intense their anxiety. In a 2008 study, Howard Berenbaum and colleagues studied people with uncertainty apprehension and discovered that their anxiety instills a deep, inflexible need for predictability and a high degree of distress when they are unable to know outcomes. If you don't know if something is going to be good, then it must be bad. If it's bad, you are likely in danger and need to be on guard, in perpetual, stressful fight-or-flight mode. If this trepidation is extreme, it can dictate our decisions and actions, limiting life and reinforcing our belief that we need to protect ourselves from unknown dangers.

Ambiguity can cause automatic negative thoughts and excessive worry. In the last chapter, we looked at anxious thought patterns such as black-and-white thinking, overgeneralizing, and jumping to conclusions. These are at work in uncertainty intolerance. When we don't know something, the anxious brain works frantically to fill in the gaps, jumping to conclusions, thinking in extremes (if it's unknown, it's terrible), and blowing things out of proportion. The mind attempts to fill in the gaps by creating all sorts of what-ifs and worst-case scenarios. In uncertainty intolerance, worry becomes a coping mechanism. Although often unintentional, worrying, fretting, and ruminating are the mind's attempts to create certainty and find answers. This anxiety is a means of self-protection, albeit misguided and ineffective.

Here's what uncertainty intolerance and accompanying anxiety might look like in a few real-life situations.

Meeting New People

This is incredibly problematic for someone with social anxiety, but anyone can experience worry when meeting someone new. Will this new colleague be tolerable to work with? Will this blind date like me? Will the teller at the bank think I'm incompetent with money when they look at my account? Is the new doctor going to think I'm a hypochondriac? In general, "I will be judged. Will I pass the test?" Unfortunately, anxiety makes us hard on ourselves, and the conclusion we jump to is usually a resounding "no." We catastrophize the consequences and worry about them until we're miserable.

Going to a Party

Parties and gatherings are often difficult for those living with anxiety, especially if uncertainty is a problem. Not knowing who will be there when you arrive, what people will be doing (Will you have to dance—with people watching?! Will that person you don't like be there, and will you have to interact? What if you have a miserable time but can't leave without looking rude? What if . . . ?). In worrying about the unknown events that might happen, it's possible to experience an entire, disastrous party in your mind before you even arrive.

Starting a New Job

New employment means new employers, new coworkers, and new tasks. What will your boss be like? What about other employees? What if you make a mistake on the first day and everyone regrets that you were hired? What if you wear the wrong thing? Say the wrong thing? Do the wrong thing? Could you lose your job on the very first day? What will that look like on your employment record? Will anyone else want to give you a job after you botch this one?

The intense need for certainty and predictability causes people to actively seek certainty, which narrows life choices and activities. At its worst, the anxiety caused by uncertainty intolerance becomes paralyzing, leading to avoidance and isolation.

Happily, it's possible to neutralize your fear of the unknown and find peace. The next section will explore how.

 When does the unknown become problematic for you? Think of situations that make you feel anxious. Could there be a component of uncertainty intolerance at work?

Uncertainty Acceptance

Because there are so many more things in life that are uncertain than are guaranteed, embracing uncertainty can make a positive difference in your anxiety level. Accepting the unpredictability and ambiguity of situations you encounter every day will allow you to let go of worry. You will no longer need to turn to worry as a coping mechanism. This greatly relieves symptoms of anxiety.

In accepting the unknown, you gift yourself with:

- Relief from the agony that comes from misguided assumptions and jumping to conclusions
- Expanded views of situations so you see multiple possibilities, not just worst-case scenarios
- Enhanced creativity and problem-solving abilities that come from thinking outside the box

Admittedly, building uncertainty tolerance and acceptance doesn't always come naturally. Remember, our brain evolved and developed to keep us safe, and it does that by watching and preparing for problems. We must gently encourage it to relax and be comfortable with not knowing. Mindfulness is instrumental in teaching ourselves to tolerate uncertainty.

Mindfulness works here because it keeps you in the only place that certainty exists—the present moment. When you live mindfully, you are fully participating in the moment, paying attention to only what is tangible, direct, and straightforward. For example, when meeting new people, going to a party, or starting a new job, you mindfully and purposefully pay attention to what is really happening in that moment. Your anxiety stays low because you don't leave the concrete present by jumping to conclusions about people or circumstances.

When you're mindful, you live your moments as they are rather than reacting based on anxious assumptions about what's happening. Mindfulness offers numerous tools to help you be present and comfortable with the uncertainty of a moment rather than trapped in something that hasn't yet begun.

Beginner's mind, acceptance, observing your behavior, and choosing your response are effective tools to use when you're anxious about life's uncertainties. To learn about these useful components of mindfulness and apply them to your own life, let's jump into a few exercises.

Embrace the Unknown

Being fully present and active in each moment can help you become less anxious about uncertainty. Try these exercises now, and return to them often for practice.

Hone Your Beginner's Mind

Someone just learning a new skill or beginning a new activity has an advantage. While beginning something involves a lot of uncertainty, someone with a beginner's mind is calm and welcoming. Rather than interpreting the new situation through past worries and fears, a beginner just lets the process unfold without judgment. This is also referred to as openness.

Close your eyes and imagine you're beginning a class, perhaps at school or at a local business, to learn about something of interest to you. Your mind might be racing with all sorts of worries and fears about what it will be like, how you will do, and whether it will be a terrible experience. To calm yourself and enjoy yourself, adopt a beginner's mind. Don't try to work out in your head what this experience will be like; rather, allow yourself to pay attention to the direct experience and what you see, smell, and hear. You are open to situations and simply live them as they are, a moment at a time.

 Reflection: Think about an upcoming situation that you're worried about. How can you approach it as a beginner rather than being full of preconceived notions and assumptions? What would that be like?

Acceptance

To accept something doesn't mean to give up or give in. When you accept something, you just let it be as it is right now without analyzing it, resisting it, reacting negatively to it, worrying about it, or avoiding it. You just take it in, experience it, and find peace in the moment.

Picture yourself back in that class. As you walk in, you notice an old acquaintance, someone you didn't get along with. You didn't realize they would be there. You start to worry about how awkward and uncomfortable the class might be. Maybe you should just leave now and never come back. Or you could accept that this person is there and concentrate on the class.

 Imagine that you stay in the class. When you accept the presence of your old acquaintance, what will you pay attention to instead? List as many possibilities as you can. What will it be like now to stay in the class?

Observe Your Behavior

Observing your behavior means being mindful of yourself. Anxiety and uncertainty about how we'll handle ourselves make us self-critical. Step back and notice (but don't judge) your emotions, thoughts, and actions. When you are a neutral observer, you can let go of predictions and judgments and simply "be."

 Return to that imaginary class. Mentally observe and describe your uncertainty- and anxiety-driven actions. Would they affect how you participate? Interact with class members? Where you sit? How long you stay? Next, think about what would be different if you had no expectations—a beginner's mind—and you just accepted the person's presence as having nothing to do with you or your experience. How would you act differently?

Choose to Respond Differently

Anxiety keeps us in reaction mode. When we are present with our worries rather than in the actual moment, we can't thoughtfully choose how we respond to problems. When we can't tolerate uncertainty, we react by avoiding, suppressing, fighting, or struggling. In so doing, we miss out on the joy and inner peace that comes from living in the now.

 You can't always choose what happens to you, but you can always choose your response. Think of that class again. How will the mindfulness skills of beginner's mind, acceptance, and observing yourself help you choose a calm, healthy response to the situation?

Changing Behavior

Changing our habits—those behaviors we repeat over and over without even realizing it—can be challenging. Because anxious reactions like worrying and avoiding can be coping mechanisms to help you deal with uncertainty intolerance, changing your responses to unknown situations might actually increase your anxiety at first.

By living mindfully in a difficult situation, you are making a huge life change and creating an entirely new uncertainty: Will the quality of your life improve or decline if you begin to put up with the unknown? For now, trust that increasing your uncertainty intolerance will decrease your anxiety. Your initial discomfort is a very normal reaction to this process. Don't give up. The more you practice mindfulness and develop your skills of beginner's mind, acceptance, observing yourself, and choosing different responses, the more your anxiety will decrease over time. You will start to notice an ease of being and sense of being okay with not knowing everything that could possibly happen in your life. Anxious thoughts will be replaced by chosen, purposeful actions. You will be free to experience, question, investigate, explore, discover, and take charge of your quality life.

Takeaways

During this week, you gained some insight into uncertainty intolerance, a big contributing factor to anxiety. You now have new information and strategies to help you decrease your apprehension about uncertainty and the worries that come with it.

- When you're apprehensive about uncertainty, anxiety limits your choices and behavior.
- To cope with uncertainty and try to fill in the blanks, the human mind worries, jumps to conclusions, catastrophizes, and thinks in extremes.
- You can drastically reduce your anxiety by teaching yourself to accept the unknown.
- Mindfulness and the tools of beginner's mind, acceptance, observing your behavior, and choosing your response lead to increased comfort with and decreased anxiety around tolerating uncertainty.

Mindful Moment—Openness to Your Moment

Begin each new day, or welcome new moments within your day, with this centering mindfulness exercise. Sit or lie down comfortably. Focus your attention on your feet, wiggling your toes and rolling your ankles, noticing how they feel. Tell yourself with conviction, "I'm open to go where my feet take me." Move your attention to your heart and your gut, noticing how they feel right now. Again, with conviction, say to yourself, "I'm open to all my different experiences today." Next, concentrate on your arms and hands and say confidently, "I embrace what is in front of me now." When your attention reaches your head, note how everything feels there and repeat, "My mind lets go of the need for control."

*I don't want to be
at the mercy of my emotions.
I want to use them,
to enjoy them,
and to dominate them.*

—**Oscar Wilde,** *The Picture of Dorian Gray*

CHAPTER FIVE

WEEK FOUR:
Dealing with Difficult Emotions

Emotions! Wouldn't it be great if we didn't have to experience them? Imagine feeling no more anxiety, fear, irritation, frustration, anger, self-doubt, or sadness. That would mean, though, that we would feel no more joy, delight, confidence, hope, curiosity, gratitude, or love. What if, then, we could experience emotions but also control them? Would we be free from the negative ones? Unfortunately, we'd be trapped just like we are now, when it seems that they dominate our lives.

No matter how strong they feel, emotions are simply feelings. They come and go. You don't have to remain at their mercy. In this chapter, we'll explore difficult emotions and learn how to simply let them hang out beside us when they appear. Having all types of emotions, enjoying the positive ones and remaining unbothered by the negative ones, is what will be great.

The Impulse to Run

As a species, we're not known for our love of discomfort. Anxiety is more than uncomfortable; it's downright miserable. Worse, it makes us feel in danger of some sort of harm, of something going wrong and ruining our lives. To protect us, our brain has a natural response: avoidance. Avoidance is part of the inborn fight-or-flight reaction to any type of harm we perceive, whether it's a product of our thoughts and emotions or a tangible threat like an attack on our life. As an instinct, "flight" is pure impulse, and the more we act on it, the more we reinforce the neural pathways in our brain that scream, "Fear! Flee!" Thus, anxiety grows, and we have more reasons to avoid. There is a difference, though, between running from a tangible threat and running from anxious thoughts and emotions.

According to a 2010 study that appeared in *Dialogues of Clinical Neurosciences*, what happens with avoidance coping in anxiety is that we have to make a decision: Do we want a possible reward, such as a joyful experience at a birthday party, or do we want to avoid difficult emotions, such as worry about having a horrible car accident on the way to that party? We perceive a threat, but because it is based on anxiety rather than imminent danger, we are able to choose our reaction. We can decide to heed the impulse to avoid, or we can choose to override it.

If you choose to run, you likely avoid difficult emotions in the short term. However, new anxiety-provoking situations pop up all the time. Avoidance worked (kind of) once, so you use that coping strategy again. And again. Soon, avoidance has become a habit that has you trapped in anxiety rather than freely enjoying life despite its discomforts. If you have found that your life is limited by anxiety and avoidance, and you're tired of choosing safety over freedom, you're in the right place to make a change. Avoidance is a reaction. You're about to learn a well-chosen response to difficult emotions.

Accept Our Anxiety

The opposite of avoidance is acceptance. Acceptance is letting your emotions simply exist alongside you, allowing them to be as they are—nothing more and nothing less. I understand that this might sound terrible, and the idea of accepting anxiety and its strong emotions might make you want to, well, avoid doing what I'm suggesting. But bear with me! Research and practice indicate that accepting negative emotions brings a sense of calm and expands your life far beyond the narrow limits imposed by anxiety.

Acceptance is an attitude, an action, and an empowering choice. It involves leaving anxiety and its negative thoughts and emotions alone and gently turning your attention to your tangible life, moment by moment. When you practice tolerance of your experiences, you give yourself the chance to feel and do things other than struggle and avoid.

First, know that acceptance does not mean assuming you'll always be anxious and giving up working for something better. It doesn't mean having to "grin and bear it." And acceptance is most definitely not resigning yourself to a bad situation. Anxiety and negative emotions can signal that something isn't right, and that's important to pay attention to. Never accept a bad situation! Accepting your feelings lets you step back and consider what you need to do to change problematic circumstances, and it frees you to do it.

So just how do you accept anxiety and its feelings and thoughts? Mindfulness is a key component of being able to live alongside worries and fears. Use these strategies in your daily life to hone acceptance.

Inviting Difficult Emotions

Monk and Zen master Thich Nhat Hanh speaks of inviting difficult thoughts and emotions for tea. When you invite your difficult emotions to do something pleasant with you, you're showing them (and yourself) that you're not afraid. When you invite anxiety to join you, you effectively remove it from inside your head and place it beside you. Then it's there but not part of you. It's not consuming you. You now have the space necessary to "drink your tea." Your emotions can grow and include pleasant feelings about your moment rather than just worries about the past and fears about the future.

Bringing Compassion to Your Emotions— and to Yourself

Because our anxious emotions are unpleasant and bothersome, we don't like them. Because they originate within our own mind, we often don't like ourselves (or at least the emotional part of ourselves). Blaming our emotions for our plight and berating ourselves for feeling the way we do only serves to make difficult emotions stronger. Part of acceptance involves being nice to yourself and your emotions, even the anxious ones. Rather than labeling them harshly and judging them as "bad," appreciate them for what they're trying to do. After all, in their own misguided way, they're looking out for you and trying to keep you safe. Acknowledging that your emotions have a purpose helps you let go of the struggle.

For those of us with anxiety, the idea of being nice to ourselves can seem strange, even undeserved. If anxiety makes you hard on yourself, you might not know how to be kind to yourself. Maybe you don't even realize that self-compassion is an option for you. Even if it feels strange or almost impossible, start treating yourself with the compassion you deserve. Why do you deserve it? Because you are you. Start small. Look in the mirror and give yourself a genuine compliment. If you immediately begin to argue with or reject your positive compliment, simply acknowledge this, and then repeat the compliment.

Your conversation might sound like this:

Your compassionate self: "I had a great conversation with my neighbor today. I'm proud that I was able to offer her a listening ear."

Your critical, anxious self: "But I think I said too much. I always talk too much. I bet she's sorry she ran into me. I'm embarrassed, mortified."

Your compassionate self: "That's just my anxiety popping up. The conversation was positive, and I'm glad. I don't have to be perfect to be helpful and likeable."

Becoming aware of your difficult emotions and how they make you self-critical will help you rise above them. You can choose how you talk to yourself, and you can be selective in what you listen to. Tune in to your self-talk, and gently guide it with kindness.

Expanding Your Possibilities in Each Moment

When we struggle against anxiety, our lives become extremely limited. To expand your experiences, pay attention mindfully to your present moment. Leave your emotions and take in your surroundings with your eyes, ears, nose, skin (touch), and taste buds (when appropriate). This shifts your attention and broadens your world in that moment.

Picture a piece of paper, blank other than a colorful dot. What will draw and keep your attention? Chances are it is the dot that you will notice and focus on. But there's so much more to that paper than the dot. There is space all around it for you to notice and fill in. That is just like the moments of your life. Anxiety is a dot in your space, but it's not your whole life. Be mindful of what is around you in any moment. What else do you see, hear, feel, smell, and taste? You don't need to get rid of the dot to enjoy everything else. Accept the dot, then mindfully shift your attention to living in the spaces.

 Try this now. On a blank page in your notebook, write one worry or anxious thought. Circle it. Then, in the space around it, brainstorm other things that you can focus on instead.

Staying off the Hook

You're not a fish, so don't get hooked! Buddhist nun, teacher, and author Pema Chödrön has written about shenpa, a Buddhist concept that means getting hooked. Anxious emotions are a part of life. On their own, they don't do much. They start to negatively impact our lives when we become hooked on them. The hook hurts (it causes life-limiting physical, emotional, and cognitive symptoms), so naturally you struggle and avoid. But imagine what it would be like if you were to accept anxiety. You could relax and simply be, floating and swimming in the "water" around you. The hook remains present in life, trying to snag you, but with mindful awareness and acceptance, you can allow it to hover while you go about your life, unhooked.

Feeling the Anxiety and Being Present Anyway

Because anxiety is so miserable, it's tempting to want it gone so you can finally start enjoying your life. Anxiety, though, is a part of the human experience. Anxious emotions and thoughts will always pop up. Allowing yourself to feel anxious frees you to move forward. Acknowledging anxiety and accepting its presence lets you live a quality life anyway.

If You're Feeling Overwhelmed

Pause for a moment. Smile, and congratulate yourself for the progress you've already made. Anxiety is stubborn, and transcending it involves hard work and patience. Sometimes, it might seem like it gets worse before it gets better. That's normal, and it's because the learning process involves reflecting on anxiety and all the difficult emotions, thoughts, and experiences that go with it. As we've seen, what you pay attention to is what grows; therefore, anxiety might seem to be growing. This can be overwhelming. Take heart. This uncomfortable stage is temporary because you're learning to place your attention elsewhere (the present moments of your real life). In the meantime, there are quick little (but ultimately very big) things you can do in an instant whenever you're feeling especially overwhelmed. Keep these strategies with you to use anytime for swift relief.

Slow, deep breathing. For mental and physical stress relief, bathe your brain in soothing, calming oxygen while expanding and relaxing the muscles of your diaphragm. Close your eyes. Inhale slowly while counting to eight (or however many slow counts it takes to fill your lungs). Hold for a few seconds, and then exhale, controlled, for a few counts longer than your inhale. Be mindful of the sound of your breath and the feel of your body. When thoughts rush in, shift your attention back to your breath. Repeat for as long as you desire.

Visualize a soothing place. Visualization is very powerful in helping us shift our emotions. What brings you a sense of inner calm? Perhaps you're comforted by sand and water, a path in a forest, a beautiful flower garden, or a favorite sunny spot in your home. Close your eyes and immerse yourself in your soothing place. What do you see? What sounds do you notice? What are its unique smells? Mentally transport yourself there and feel your muscles let go and relax. If your anxiety tags along, just accept it and let it walk beside you, but give your attention to your surroundings.

Aromatherapy. Have you ever caught a whiff of something and instantly been transported back in time to vividly experience a memory? Our sense of smell is incredibly potent. The molecules in scent travel to the olfactory bulbs in the brain and from there directly to emotional and memory centers, including the amygdala. Therefore, we can stimulate and influence our emotions through scents, a practice called aromatherapy. Using a diffuser to disperse the chemicals of smells into your space can keep you feeling centered. Lavender, chamomile, bergamot, cedarwood, and cilantro are just a few plants whose properties are known to calm anxiety and stress.

Drink decaf tea. Mindfully sipping tea is a pleasant way to feel calm and at peace. The warmth of the tea, the healthy properties of the leaves, and the experience of sitting and relaxing help relieve negative emotions. Caffeine is known to increase anxiety, so stick with white, herbal, and rooibos teas. If you can't spare time to take a break and have one-on-one time with your tea, drinking it while doing something else can still be helpful. Just be fully present and savor the experience every time you take a sip.

Ground yourself. This one is very quick yet still helpful. When you notice your anxiety spike and your negative emotions start to overwhelm you, plant both feet firmly on the ground, place your hands palms-down on your lap or other surface, and/or hold an object in your hands. Place your attention on your feet or hands and feel them connect with something solid. Remind yourself that what is real is what you can touch and feel right now.

Replace negative thoughts with positive ones. Negative thoughts and emotions can be so automatic that they run constantly in the background, negative mental chatter that keeps you anxious. When you notice a limiting thought or feeling, immediately replace it with something more realistic and positive. For example, "Everyone hates me" becomes "I'm having the thought that everyone hates me. In reality, my friend Betty likes me for who I am. So does Tom at work. And the woman who rings up my groceries at my favorite store always lights up when she sees me, and we have great conversations."

Panic Attacks

In this section, we'll explore panic, or anxiety, attacks to help you understand what's happening to you during one and learn ways to cope with them while they're occurring. If you don't experience panic attacks, feel free to skip this section.

As you learned in chapter 1, panic attacks can be part of panic disorder, a fear of having panic attacks in public. Anxiety attacks are sudden bursts of gripping anxiety that are triggered by thoughts, emotions, or other stressors. The terms are often used interchangeably, so I'll use them both here. Whatever they're called, they are sudden and severe experiences of high anxiety that involve forceful emotions, thoughts, and physical sensations that stop you in your tracks, causing life as you know it to temporarily come to a screeching halt.

Understanding what's happening during a panic attack can help it feel less scary and allow you to regain control more quickly.

Triggers

Panic attacks can seem to happen out of the blue, with no apparent cause (the trigger is usually subconscious, below your awareness), or they can be triggered by something known and specific: being in the same place you once had a panic attack or high anxiety about a looming meeting at work, for example. In either case, your brain picks up signals that it interprets as danger. You react in an instant, and your anxiety is all-encompassing, affecting mind, body, thoughts, feelings, and behaviors. Identifying and understanding your triggers can allow you to work on reducing your anxiety about these panic attack causes.

Physical Manifestations

You can feel panic attacks throughout your entire body because your brain shuts down your parasympathetic nervous system—the calm one—and revs up the sympathetic nervous system—the reactive, alert one. You're being prepared to fight for your life or run for it. Blood is instantly diverted from your organs to your skeletal muscles. Your heart rate and blood pressure skyrocket, and your lungs work too quickly as they try to supply oxygen to fuel this reaction. As a result, you might hyperventilate. You might be in pain anywhere and everywhere. You'll likely tremble and sweat. You could feel and become physically ill. Many people describe the physical experience of panic as the worst feeling they've ever had.

Psychological Distress

Panic attacks scare people to pieces. When you think you are dying, all your thoughts and feelings are going to react negatively. Anxiety attacks usurp your sense of control over yourself and your life. Anxiety causes panic attacks, and panic attacks significantly increase anxiety, fear, and worry. People often report feeling like they're going crazy or losing control. To ease this horrific sensation, people often change their behavior to avoid experiencing panic attacks again. Unfortunately, this means worry about these attacks remains high, which increases the likelihood of future anxiety attacks.

Coping with Panic Attacks

Triggered by something (even if it's unknown to you and thus unexpected), panic attacks are very real experiences that happen within your mind and body. They feel real because real physical and psychological events are occurring, but these strong bursts of anxiety are not your reality. They're not who you are, and they don't represent your life. Your life takes place in the tangible world rather than in the fear you might currently be trapped in; therefore, the tools of mindfulness can help you cope with panic attacks when they happen. Over time, they'll even reduce the frequency and intensity of the attacks. The following tools have been found to be particularly helpful with panic attacks.

Awareness. Get to know your anxiety attacks. Consider keeping a journal to record what you were thinking, feeling, and doing before a panic attack occurred. Look for patterns to identify your triggers. The more aware of your triggers you are, the more you can address them, overcome the anxiety they cause, and prevent panic.

Self-compassion. Too often, people beat themselves up for having anxiety attacks. Not only does this perpetuate negative emotions and thoughts, but it is wholly unjustified. Panic attacks aren't weakness. They don't mean you can't handle your life. They are nothing more than your physical brain and body's reaction to a trigger. It's not much different than, say, hunger. Your brain is triggered by a lack of calories and nutrients, so it starts a physical and emotional reaction to being hungry. Hunger isn't a weakness, and despite how we say it in English, you "aren't" hungry. You "have" hunger (that's how they say it in Spanish). Catch your negative thoughts and emotions about yourself, and replace them with positive, realistic ones (this is a theme in untangling anxiety). Remind yourself that you are reacting involuntarily to a trigger. That's it. Then pause and appreciate one of your many strengths.

Acceptance. In this chapter, we've talked a lot about acceptance because it is an incredibly effective mindfulness tool that frees you from struggling against anxiety—and panic, too. When you feel panic begin, step back from it by accepting the sensations rather than struggling to stop them. Remind yourself that, despite the illusion, you are safe and alive (you're not dying). Acceptance shortens the duration and intensity of anxiety attacks.

Relaxation techniques. Panic attacks involve our entire physical body, from the nervous systems to our organs to our muscles and joints. The more aware you are of the physical sensations that signal that your body is reacting to a trigger, the more you can calm the reaction through relaxation techniques. When you recognize the onset of panic, engage in deep breathing and grounding to induce calm. Then, when panic has subsided, try progressive muscle relaxation to feel better faster. Starting with your toes and gradually reaching the top of your head, tighten groups of muscles, hold for a few seconds, and release. You'll let go of stress and tension.

Support groups. While technically not a mindfulness activity (you can participate in them mindfully, of course), seeking support from other people who experience panic attacks can be very helpful. Hearing others' stories and sharing your own enhances a sense of connection and helps you stop being so hard on yourself (after all, you're not alone in this terrible experience). You can also exchange strategies for dealing with and overcoming panic attacks and generally reducing anxiety.

Anxiety attacks and all negative, anxious emotions are things you experience, but they don't have to remain a permanent part of your life. Approach them mindfully to begin to loosen the grip they have on you and free yourself to live a quality life you create.

Takeaways

Congratulations on making it through a hard week! Celebrate your accomplishment by intentionally doing something nice for yourself and being mindful while doing it. Go for a brisk walk around the block, dance to peppy music, buy yourself flowers, engage in a fun activity with loved ones, or do anything that makes you feel good about yourself. Dealing with the difficult emotions that accompany anxiety can be tough, but it's worth it. This week you learned:

- How avoidance not only is ineffective but actually increases anxiety
- A mindfulness strategy called acceptance and how to use it to release yourself from the negative emotions of anxiety
- The ways in which panic attacks are all-encompassing, gripping, and restricting
- Tools for dealing with panic attacks in the moment and beyond so you can gradually reduce their presence in your life

Mindful Moment—Scribble It Out Joyfully

Find a pleasant, comfortable place to spend a few (or many) moments. Grab a blank sheet of paper and some colored pencils, markers, crayons, or just different colored pens. Turn on some inspirational, peppy, or relaxing music (classical or jazz are great choices for this exercise, but the best music is what you enjoy). As you listen to the music, scribble or draw to the beat. Immerse yourself completely in the experience, and when anxious thoughts intrude, just accept their presence without tangling with them. Don't worry about creating a product. Simply doodle mindfully to the music.

*People become attached to
their burdens sometimes
more than the burdens
are attached to them.*

—George Bernard Shaw

CHAPTER SIX

WEEK FIVE:
Sticky Thoughts

The Pike Place Market in Seattle boasts a large gum wall. It is like a gigantic mural along the length of the building's exterior, but it isn't painted. It consists of wads upon wads of chewed gum. It's sticky, so people put stuff on it (business cards, pictures, and more). Sometimes, our brain is like one gigantic gum wall, so sticky that it attracts our negative thoughts and holds them tightly in place. We're not free to move effortlessly, and we remain stuck in anxiety, unable to take effective action to overcome it. Two of the biggest, juiciest, stickiest pieces of gum that are obstacles in the way of overcoming anxiety are procrastination and worry. This week, we'll examine the anxious thoughts behind them. Consider this a tool, a scraper, for removing them from your brain, your wall.

Procrastination

Many people are surprised to learn that procrastination is closely tied to anxiety. It's a form of avoidance, our innate impulse to run away from anxiety-provoking, safety-compromising situations. Avoiding something until the last minute rather than diving right in is both a cause and an effect of anxiety.

If you're anxious about a task in front of you, such as calling someone on the phone (if you have social anxiety, you might loathe the phone like I once did) or completing a project for work or school, you might deal with it by ignoring it and finding a bunch of other, smaller, less important undertakings. This isn't weakness or laziness. It's procrastination, a defense mechanism that allows you some temporary relief from your anxiety because you are ignoring what's in front of you and turning to something else.

Procrastination can cause anxiety because it increases the pressure of time, makes things more urgent than they need to be, and adds an undue amount of stress to our lives. The more we procrastinate, the more we risk failing in what we're doing. (Ironically, the fear of failure is often what causes procrastination in the first place.) Rather than relieving anxiety, procrastination adds new layers onto it, such as:

- Increased worry and fear of failure
- A risk of health problems if you're avoiding making an appointment with a doctor to check a scary symptom
- Loss of sleep, which exacerbates anxiety
- Unhealthy lifestyle habits (scrambling to do something at the last minute often makes it so people don't have time to exercise or make healthy meals)
- Decreased performance on the job or in your relationships
- Negative emotions such as guilt and shame
- Decreased sense of well-being
- Increased negative thought patterns such as catastrophizing and jumping to conclusions (believing that facing your task will be a disaster and that you are sure to fail)

Procrastination and anxiety negatively affect life by dominating our thoughts and emotions and preventing positive action.

Consider these important elements:

Fear of Failure

Fear of failure is one of the biggest factors underlying procrastination. It's tied to performance anxiety, perfectionism, and social anxiety. The thought of failing in any way can lead to anxiety so paralyzing that it's almost impossible to start a project or take action toward a goal. Anxious, negative thought patterns that make us stick to our starting block include:

Black-and-white (or all-or-nothing) thinking: "If I'm not perfect, I'm worthless, a failure."

Catastrophizing: "If I can't be the perfect partner, my significant other will stop loving me and our relationship will fail."

Mind reading: "My boss will hate the report I put together. I'll never get an opportunity to advance."

Each of these anxious thoughts about failing can keep you locked in place, unable or unwilling to engage in valuable activities that could enhance the quality of your life.

Information Overload

If you have something that you need to do—an assignment, a work task, a home-improvement project, a health concern you need to investigate, a car you want to buy—technology provides access to a wealth of information any time you need it. While this is largely good, it can contribute to anxiety and cause us to procrastinate. Having too much information about anything, especially when the information is conflicting, is overwhelming and anxiety-provoking. It can seem impossible to begin to sort through it all to find something meaningful, and it's tempting to put off doing so. Types of sticky, anxious thoughts that prevent us from progressing when we have information overload include:

Magnification: "This is way too much. I can't possibly deal with this. I've failed, and I haven't even started."

Emotional reasoning: "I'm overwhelmed. I clearly can't handle my class/job/relationship/life."

Intolerance of Uncertainty

In chapter 4, we explored uncertainty intolerance and its role in anxiety. Intolerance of uncertainty rears its ugly head here, too. There's a lot of uncertainty involved in starting something new. Will you like it, or will you hate it? What if you hate it? Once you start, will it be too late to back out? Regardless of how you feel about it, what if something goes wrong? What if the consequences are terrible? What if you make that appointment with your doctor to check out that persistent cough and you find out it's lung cancer? Is not knowing better than knowing?

Among the negative thought patterns that prevent you from starting something or taking an important action are:

Jumping to conclusions: "I don't know what might happen; therefore, it might be bad, and I should avoid it."

Dwelling on the negative: "No matter how many good things could happen, bad things could happen, too. I need to protect myself."

Bad Habit

Unfortunately, procrastination leads to more procrastination. It does serve as a defense mechanism that protects us from what we think might happen if we pursue something, but it becomes a vicious cycle. Thoughts influence our actions (we think we might fail, for example, so we put off starting something). Actions, in turn, influence our thoughts. Delaying facing something allows us to avoid anxiety for a short time, so the brain learns that procrastination makes us more comfortable. The next time we face something difficult to start, the brain remembers that procrastination brought some relief, so we do it again. Procrastination can become a bad habit that is hard to break.

Overcome Procrastination

Procrastination has a purpose. It is a strategy (albeit ultimately ineffective and more anxiety-provoking) to relieve stress and worry about a difficult task on your to-do list. It helps you regulate your mood and your thoughts about the task. Now that you're aware of its function, you can replace it with a different, more useful strategy. One of the best ways to face what's in front of you is mindfulness, and it's a great alternative to procrastination.

Anxiety causes you to procrastinate, which helps you avoid what you think are negative consequences of diving into the task at hand. Unfortunately, in the long run, procrastination causes more anxiety than it relieves. There can be negative consequences to putting off important tasks. Failing to meet deadlines or ignoring medical problems when they could still be caught early, for example, can have dire consequences for your life.

Mindfulness, on the other hand, is living life as it is happening, being open to all possibilities, and embracing what is. Mindfulness pulls you out of hiding and plops you into the present moment where your task awaits. Being present, keeping your attention on what is right here, right now, frees you from your sticky, gummy, anxious thoughts. Mindfulness doesn't magically make a difficult task disappear, but what it does do is equip you to face it. Facing it and completing it are what will ultimately untangle you from your anxiety about it.

The following actions will help you overcome your anxiety about your difficult task. Do them mindfully, with your thoughts and emotions attending to each task as you engage. Your action combined with mindfulness will allow you to complete the task and further reduce anxiety.

 Your notebook can be a handy tool during this exercise.

Make a list and prioritize. Purposefully think about what you must do to complete what you're facing. List all steps you need to take. Then examine them. Break them down further into even smaller pieces. Once you have your list of manageable tasks, organize it into order of importance. What is the number one thing you need to do in this moment to get started? Pay attention only to this. Moment by moment, step by step, you'll march toward your finish line.

Start somewhere. Not all projects are linear, with steps that must be done in order. Sometimes, the best thing to do is identify one part of your project and do it right now. Don't worry about what still lies ahead or what you think you should be doing instead. Just pick a starting point and go. When you've finished, pause and immerse yourself in the feeling of accomplishment that you'll undoubtedly experience. Both the action and allowing yourself to own it will carry you to the next step.

Temper your expectations. Our expectations often interfere with reality. Reality is objective. It's factual. When we are anchored in reality and all its present moments, projects aren't nearly as daunting. However, when all-too-human expectations jump into the mix, problems can arise.

For example, say you're getting married and planning the wedding. Of course, you want it to be nice, but expecting extravagance or perfection can lead to anxiety about the event, and then procrastination. You'll be more prone to worry about what-ifs, worst-case scenarios, and disappointments. These thoughts will interfere with your ability to plan your special day. You might even shut down, creating more angst about your wedding. Creating realistic expectations is an important step in freeing yourself to do what's necessary.

Reward yourself. In human behavior, incentive theory posits that we're motivated by the promise of rewards. While too simple to completely explain why we behave the way we do, when it comes to anxiety and procrastination, incentives can help us get going. Rather than remaining mired in worries and fears, give yourself some motivation. Treat yourself upon completing part of your task or to-do list. You might work on a hobby you enjoy or read a book. Put on music and dance happily. Walk in the sunshine. Knowing you get to do something enjoyable when you've met part of your goal—and then doing it mindfully, fully experiencing it—releases dopamine and endorphins and replaces anxious thoughts with confident, satisfied ones. Doing this repeatedly decreases the habit of procrastination because rewards reinforce positive behavior.

Adopt routines and tools. A powerful success strategy in businesses, schools, and homes everywhere is to create and follow routines. When you have a set schedule and structure to your day, it's easier to know what to do and when to do it. Dedicating a specific time frame to tackle your to-do list helps you stick to it. Plan both a start and an end time to keep you focused and positive; when you know you will be able to stop at a concrete time, it's easier to begin work and focus while doing so. Also, equip yourself with what you need to get the job done. Setting yourself up for success reduces anxiety and minimizes opportunities for procrastination.

Learn to delegate. Thinking that all aspects of a big project are completely on your shoulders is stressful and daunting. It's hard to start climbing a mountain when you have no support team. Sometimes, anxiety makes it hard to ask for help, but avoiding doing so can keep you at the starting line. Before reaching out, decide what you most need help with. Then offer one of those tasks to someone. Don't think of it as imposing or admitting weakness; instead, acknowledge it for what it is: You are giving someone else an opportunity to succeed, and in so doing, you're being a leader as well as doing what it takes to get the thing done.

Learn by trying. Self-efficacy is the belief that you are capable of doing something. A major cause of procrastination is the lack of this part of your self-concept. This relates to the fear of failure we explored earlier. Focusing on what you perceive to be your limitations causes anxiety. That anxiety can stop you before you even start. Think of yourself as a beginner and give yourself permission to not know. The way we learn best is by doing. By trying, goofing up, going back to the drawing board, and trying again, you and your abilities grow. Tackle your tasks and to-dos like a beginner and allow yourself to try, and try again.

Don't blame yourself. Procrastination and anxiety have a partner, and its name is guilt. When anxiety prevents you from taking necessary action toward a goal, you might feel guilty and berate yourself, even calling yourself some harsh names in the process. However, if you procrastinate, you're probably not doing so because you love putting off what you're supposed to be doing. More likely, you care about the outcome, and worry and fear are paralyzing you. Remind yourself of your strengths and apply mindfulness: rather than being stuck in the future (what you haven't yet done), focus on what you are doing right now to move toward your goal.

Underlying procrastination is the "w" word that underlies every component of anxiety: worry.

Worry

The words "worry" and "anxiety" are often used interchangeably, for good reason. While anxiety is a bit broader than worry and encompasses our entire experience (mind, body, spirit, perspective, and behavior), worry is at its core. In fact, worry is the primary component of every anxiety disorder. Even if you are plagued by anxiety but don't have a diagnosable disorder, chances are very high that worry is playing too big a part in your life.

Worry is a normal human emotion experienced, from time to time, by 100 percent of people. We worry because we care about someone or something. You wouldn't worry about a loved one's safety if you didn't care about their life. You wouldn't worry about money if you didn't care about having a roof over your head and enough healthy food to eat. Occasional worry is a sign that you value yourself, others, and life itself. So, if you're a worrier, take a step back and appreciate that one of your core character strengths and virtues is your ability to love and care.

When worry is healthy, it can be motivating, helping us behave in positive ways that keep ourselves and others safe, well, and thriving. Worry can easily spiral out of control, however, and shut us down. It can tangle us up in what-ifs and worst-case scenarios, and we become prisoners of our own minds. Imagined consequences make even small problems grow so enormous that we can't escape them. Instead of living and acting in our actual world, we are trapped in our anxious thoughts and feelings about perceived problems. Worries cover up our inner windows and doors, blocking our reality, so we see, hear, and experience only our anxiety. Then it's much harder to take positive action to confront our worries, enjoy the people we care about, and live the life we value.

Worth the Worry

One of the ways in which anxiety makes life difficult is that it makes you think that everything is equally worth worrying about. When anxious thoughts dominate, everything seems like a disaster. Everything, therefore, is worthy of your concern. Anxious worry can make the mightiest mountain out of the tiniest molehill. When worry consumes us, our view is blocked by high, jagged, barren mountains. (They're barren because they're devoid of our real life.) Simply realizing that anxiety is tricking you into thinking that every thought you have is worth worrying about is the first step in scaling your worry mountains.

Worry Triggers

Worry triggers are the things we think are worth our time and energy to ruminate about. In any type of anxiety, worry becomes an instant reaction to things we think, feel, see, or otherwise encounter. Your worry triggers are unique to you. Knowing what they are allows you to recognize them, catch yourself worrying, and start pulverizing your mountains back to their molehill size.

Lace up your climbing-and-stomping boots, wiggle your toes in them, and notice what it feels like to begin to empower yourself. You're about to engage in some mindfulness exercises to help you begin to see, breathe, and live beyond your worries.

Working Through Worry

We get tangled in worry when it blocks our view of everything else. Ordering yourself to stop worrying doesn't work because your focus remains on anxiety. The most effective way to work through worry isn't to resist worrying but to expand your thoughts, feelings, and actions. Mindfulness is an ideal approach, for it shifts and broadens your perspective. Rather than focusing on a worry trigger, you fully exist where you are right now. Gently turning your thoughts away from worries shows your mind that there are other things in your world worth your attention. Use these three exercises to help yourself through moments of intense worry:

 Use your notebook to deepen your experience and get your responses out of your head and onto paper where you can see them and better address them.

Move away from worry. When you find yourself fretting, simply pause and breathe deeply. Note your thoughts. Let them exist without fueling them or fighting with them, and then shift yourself elsewhere. Physically move to a different location if you can, and if you can't, then visualize your worries moving away from you. Mentally, physically, or both, create distance between yourself and your worries. Pay attention to your surroundings instead of your thoughts, and actively do something where you physically are to occupy your time and energy. Keep yourself present and your worries removed from your personal space. Remind yourself, "I am here now. My worries are over there. They aren't with me, so I am free to think and do other things."

Express your feelings. When we keep our worries bottled up inside, they can't get out. When they can't get out, they grow bigger and louder—much like a dog stuck inside who barks and whines incessantly if he wants to go outside. Often, expressing your feelings in a way that works for you provides immediate relief from anxiety, plus it has a long-term benefit—it gets your worries out of your head and in front of you where you can effectively deal with them. Some helpful, healthy, mindful ways to express your feelings include journaling (devote 5 or 10 minutes every day to writing down and reflecting on your worries), talking with a friend or partner, or engaging in physical exercise (for many people, movement and sweat express worry better than words can). Experiment to find what helps you express your feelings. Then do it regularly to free yourself.

Examine your worries. By nature, anxiety is chaotic. Worries, while strong and overpowering, can seem vague and out of control. Regain your power over your own mind by reining in your worries. When your worries are intense, sit down with them mindfully. Invite them to be with you while you create a pleasant moment. Sit in a comfortable chair in a place you enjoy. Sip some tea, coffee (but anxiety feeds on caffeine, so keep your daily caffeine consumption as low as possible), or even water, and listen to your worries. Pluck out one that is particularly bothersome and consider it rationally. Ask yourself the following questions:

- What is most upsetting to you?
- Why?
- If the worry came true, what is the worst that would happen?
- How would you survive and thrive anyway?
- What little steps can you take, starting now, to keep the worry from coming true?

By being present with your worries in this way, you quiet the chaos and swim purposefully rather than drown in overwhelming anxiety.

Using mindfulness to replace worrying with better thoughts and behaviors is absolutely within your reach, no matter how long you've been worrying and regardless of how many things you worry about. It works because it allows you to continue to care about who and what is important to you. You're letting go of worry as an automatic reaction and developing the skill of living fully and responding to life lovingly and openly.

Takeaways

Wiggle your fingers and toes. Now picture your brain wiggling its figurative little fingers and toes, too. How does it feel to be a little less sticky? As you continue to apply what you've learned in this chapter, your anxious thoughts will no longer hold you captive, and you'll become much freer and clearer in both your thoughts and actions. Keep these key takeaways with you to keep yourself unstuck:

- When anxious, our brain tends to be sticky like chewed gum, attracting and holding on to worries and restricting our actions through procrastination.
- The anxiety behind procrastination involves fear of failure, information overload, and intolerance of uncertainty, and it can plague us so much that procrastination becomes a habit.
- Action is the key to overcoming procrastination, and mindful presence and behavior help you get going and keep moving forward.
- Worry can be overpowering and keep us stuck in place. The more you understand your worry, the more you empower yourself to move past it.
- Work through your worry intentionally and mindfully. Doing the exercises you learned in this chapter often will free you to live your life unencumbered by anxiety.

Mindful Moment—Not Knowing, Not Sticking, Not Fearing

Settle into a pleasant, comfortable space. Sit quietly and breathe. Pay attention to how your breath sounds and feels. Let thoughts come and go, neither forcing them to appear nor pushing them away. Accept your anxious thoughts without judging them or sticking with them. Respond to each thought by saying, "That's just one of many possibilities." Say nothing more or nothing less. Do this for 5 to 10 minutes, and feel free to adjust the time. When the time is up, smile and be proud of yourself for engaging in your present moment this way rather than tangling with the thoughts that popped up.

Your body hears everything
your mind says.

—Naomi Judd

CHAPTER SEVEN

WEEK SIX:
Being in Your Body

If anxiety were simply a matter of thoughts in our head, we wouldn't need this chapter. However, as you're about to explore, the mind and body don't exist as separate entities. We are one complete whole. Dr. Deepak Chopra, world-renowned healing expert, calls our "self" the bodymind. At our very core and down to the molecular level, our thoughts, feelings, physical body, total system, and communication within that system are one whole entity. Science is understanding this more and more with every new study. This heightened understanding is shown in emerging language and concepts that describe our health—mental and physical—as one entity.

- The immune system has been dubbed our "floating brain."
- The gut is often referred to as our "second brain" and our "third nervous system" (the central nervous system and the peripheral nervous system have long been identified as our two primary nervous systems) or "enteric nervous system" because it has over 100 million nerves that coordinate digestion and communicate continually with the brain. You might be surprised to learn that a significant amount of serotonin, the neurotransmitter important in regulating mood, is made in the gut, not the brain.
- Our thoughts (including worries), emotions (including fears), beliefs, and memories are, by nature, chemical and electrical signals zooming through our brain and body.

Our anxiety isn't just in the mind or the brain. It is experienced by our entire being, and as a result, we feel very real physical symptoms. Your journey this week involves being fully present in your body to heal anxiety on a deep level. The more aware you are of anxiety in your body, the better able you'll be to address it and feel better throughout your entire bodymind.

When Anxiety Floods Your Body

Anxiety is a product of our thoughts. As you now know, our thoughts aren't always true; knowing this is an effective way to keep anxiety in perspective. It can be hard to remember that, though, when the product of our thoughts is distributed and nurtured throughout the rest of our body. (If you peek back at chapter 1, you can revisit how anxiety is embedded in many body systems and parts.)

In her quote at the start of this chapter, Judd is correct: your body hears everything your mind so much as whispers, and it reacts to everything happening in the brain both molecularly and chemically. These reactions can make us physically miserable. Everyone is unique, so your own physical symptoms will differ from another's. However, because of the nature of our bodymind, everyone feels anxiety somewhere in the body. Here are just some of the ways anxiety is kept alive in our body.

Headaches. Headaches are a very common manifestation of anxiety. Stress and anxiety can be responsible for migraines, tension headaches, vascular headaches, and traction headaches. Each type feels a little different than the others, but they're all painful and reduce your quality of life.

Light-headedness. Feeling light-headed or dizzy is a complaint of many people with anxiety. It can happen upon standing or shifting positions abruptly or be a prolonged experience.

Difficulty breathing. Anxiety can cause tension and soreness in the muscles of the diaphragm, making it difficult or even painful to take a deep breath. This, in turn, reduces oxygen levels in the blood, which makes anxiety spike even higher. Panic attacks sometimes result.

Chest pain. Anxiety can mimic heart attacks. Shooting, heart-clutching pain is scary, which fuels more anxiety, panic, and pain.

Sweating. Much to the chagrin of people with social anxiety (because of their fear that others will see this visible sign of anxiety), any type of anxiety can cause people to sweat mildly or profusely.

Joint pain. While vague but very noticeable, persistent aches and pains throughout the body do occur. Anxiety can trigger an inflammatory response in the immune system, potentially damaging many body systems. When the inflammation triggers the joints, pain results.

Difficulty swallowing and/or choking sensations. The entire digestive system can be impacted by anxiety. You can feel anxiety in your throat, making it hard to swallow. You might even feel like you're choking. This scary experience can lead to more anxiety and panic attacks.

Nausea and/or abdominal pain. The nerves in the gut as well as the organs and muscles are very susceptible to stress and anxiety. Pain and nausea, and even vomiting, often occur with anxiety.

Diarrhea and/or constipation. Anxiety can lead to changes in bowel habits. It can even cause or worsen a medical condition known as irritable bowel syndrome.

Fatigue. Stress and anxiety wreak havoc on us, revving us up over and over again throughout the day in response to triggers, including our own thoughts. This is exhausting and, along with anxiety-induced sleep disruptions, causes extreme tiredness.

Paresthesia. This is the medical term for numbness and tingling. Anxiety can cause pins-and-needles sensations in the hands and feet.

Colds/flus. If you find yourself frustratingly battling cold after cold, unable to fully recover, anxiety might be to blame. Chronic worry has been found to compromise our immune system.

Emerging research finds that anxiety causes physical symptoms and even illnesses. It can worsen existing medical conditions, too. If you experience any physical symptoms, it's important to get them checked by your doctor to rule out other causes.

The Mind-Body Connection

On its own the body knows how to survive. It's up to us to teach it to thrive.
—Deepak Chopra and Rudolph E. Tanzi, **The Healing Self**

Medical- and mental-health professionals often speak of the mind-body connection. While this term is an important one and conveys the idea that we are one unified whole, it doesn't quite do justice to the concept. Deepak Chopra explains the term's limitation aptly by using the metaphor of a bridge versus telephone lines. Our connection is much more than a bridge linking two separate riverbanks; the mind and body aren't separate entities linked by a static passage. Instead, we are a system of phone lines or fiber-optic cables. Those transmission channels are filled with messages speeding through the brain, nervous systems, muscles, joints, organs, blood, and everything else, down to the tiniest component of the tiniest cell.

Further, the body isn't a passive thing that stuff happens to. We now know that the brain isn't the only organ that creates, houses, and uses neurotransmitters. These molecules, essential to our function and intra-system communication, are found, and even produced, throughout the body. For this reason, anxiety and its symptoms, effects, thoughts, and emotions can run rampant within the "telephone lines" that connect our mind and body as one complete whole.

Deepak Chopra and Rudolf Tanzi explain in *The Healing Self* that:

> *"Mind" is spread throughout your body. A heart or liver cell doesn't think in words and sentences, but it sends and receives complex chemical messages all the time. The bloodstream, along with the central nervous system, is an information superhighway, teeming with traffic as 50 trillion cells contribute to a unified goal: remaining alive, healthy, and thriving.*

Unfortunately, anxiety is a gigantic roadblock on this mind-body superhighway. Anxiety interferes with our natural drive to be mentally and physically healthy and to thrive in the quality life we create for ourselves.

The great news for our health and well-being is that we can harness the power of our mind-body connection to extract ourselves from anxiety and heal our entire being. The purpose of mindfulness is to bring us in touch with what is happening in our minds and bodies as well as with the world around us. This awareness leads to harmony with ourselves, others, and situations in our lives. Living mindfully doesn't change our circumstances. It does something much better than that. It creates positive changes in our bodymind. Rather than becoming mentally and physically ill in reaction to anxiety triggers, we respond peacefully and calmly. Mindfulness nurtures our mind-body connection, our bodymind, to allow us to thrive in all circumstances of our lives.

Mindful Movement

Rooted in India, yoga is the ancient and modern practice of focusing the mind to direct the flow of energy in the body. Yoga is a Sanskrit word meaning "union," and it captures its purpose: to bring the mind, body, and spirit into harmony. The late Chögyam Trungpa, a renowned Buddhist teacher and pioneer of introducing mindfulness and meditation to the Western world, taught that calming anxiety (and ourselves) works best when the body and mind are synchronized. When we practice yoga, a powerful form of mindful movement, we do this for ourselves.

If, like me, you have less physical flexibility than an iron rod, take heart. You don't have to do any of those superhuman poses that show up on calendars!

Mindfully engage in this simple yoga sequence anytime you need to calm anxiety:

1. Stand with your feet hip-width apart and your arms loosely at your sides.
2. Inhale slowly and deeply, and gently raise your arms overhead.
3. Pause and hold your breath for a few seconds.
4. Gradually, with control, exhale and bend forward, eventually letting your fingertips touch the ground. If they don't reach the ground, you can rest them on a yoga block, a pillow, a folded blanket, or your legs. Be sure to keep your knees bent comfortably to protect your back and prevent injury.
5. Lower yourself down to all fours, pause, and take several slow, deep breaths.
6. Inhale as you drop your belly and look up. Pause.
7. Exhale as you round your back and tuck your chin.
8. Return to a neutral, flat-back position on all fours and notice how you feel throughout your body.

Cultivate Body Awareness

Our bodymind will always be connected in a circuit of high-speed chemical and electrical messages. Despite the uncomfortable physical symptoms you might be experiencing now, this is great news for you and your anxiety! It means that you can calm your anxiety and free yourself from it by addressing both your mind and body. A powerful way to do just that is through mindfulness, a way of being that involves cultivating awareness of our whole bodymind.

Being mindful of yourself means turning inward and quietly listening, without judging or trying to change the signals your body is sending you. To do this, focus your attention on your body, one area at a time, and just note how you feel. Doing this offers many benefits:

It quiets your mind. With anxiety, the mind is hardly ever still. It races with worries, what-ifs, and worst-case scenarios. Pausing to reconnect with your whole being diverts your attention and calms your mind.

You can turn inward and scan your body wherever you are no matter what you are doing. If you are in a meeting at work, in line at the grocery store, or stuck in a traffic jam, when you notice stress and anxiety taking over, pause and attend to your body. Mindfully scan from toe to head, pausing in each area to simply notice. Your mind can't race anxiously while you are turning inward and becoming present with yourself.

You learn about your body's unique response to anxiety and stress. This is much more valuable to you than memorizing a generic list of anxiety symptoms. Know your personal reactions so you can tailor your responses to what you need most.

Look for patterns as you do this exercise throughout each day. Where do you feel well despite anxiety? Where is stress making you feel subpar? Dote on your problem areas to nurture them back to health.

You discover where you are most tense. Everyone holds tension in different places and ways. When you are aware of your body, you can concentrate your efforts to release tension precisely where you need to do so the most.

When you identify sore, tense spots, spend extra time there. Massage any knots to loosen them and focus your attention on the area as you breathe to relax.

It helps you nurture self-compassion for your body and its cues. So many of us become hard on ourselves when we're anxious and stressed. Our instant response to our physical symptoms of anxiety is often irritation, impatience, or even anger. We don't need these physical challenges added on to anxiety, and we want to shove them aside. Unfortunately, becoming frustrated serves only to maintain those symptoms and increase anxiety.

Your body is you. Know yourself completely and learn how your body tells your mind what it needs. Rather than being hard on yourself because of your anxiety and its symptoms, cultivate awareness.

With awareness, you become compassionate and more loving toward yourself. That alone goes far in reducing anxiety and helping you feel better.

Breaking Autopilot

When we're tangled up in anxiety, we're essentially trapped in our own head and consumed by anxious thoughts, emotions, and physical sensations. If anxiety has you trapped this way, you might be living on autopilot. Do you move around without really experiencing anything to its fullest? Do you do things without thinking because they're dictated by your anxiety?

Perhaps you might recognize pieces of yourself in Jada, a woman whose anxiety tries to trap her in bed every single morning because she is filled with dread for the day ahead.

Jada screeches out of her garage and drives to work in a rush, berating herself for taking so long to get up and going again this morning. As she drives, her thoughts turn to the terrible things she will face at work. Suddenly and to her surprise, she finds herself in the parking lot. Other than all the maddening red lights and congested traffic, she doesn't remember the drive. She angrily wipes her eyes as she lurches into the first parking space she sees. She absently rubs her hands and is confused about why they ache. She must have been gripping the steering wheel too hard. Her body hurts as she steps out of the car, but she ignores how she feels. She hurries in, plops down at her desk, boots up her computer, and begins leafing through a stack of papers that wasn't there last night. (Or was it? She doesn't remember.) She reaches into her desk for the antacids and aspirin. She trots to the break room, pours a cup of coffee to chase down the aspirin, and rushes out. She stops short. She just realized that Linda and Malik were in the room. Did they say something to her? Did she inadvertently snub them? With a worried sigh, she returns to her desk to dig into that stack of papers.

If you recognized yourself in Jada's story, consumed by anxious thoughts and simply going through the motions to get through your day, it can be better. You don't have to keep living on autopilot, missing moments. With awareness and mindfulness, you can begin to live fully and be present in your life.

 Start with awareness. Begin to pay attention to your anxiety and what it's doing to you. Identify just one thing that is bothering you. (At first, I had a hard time choosing just one thing to change, but trying to take on too much at once leads to frustration and more anxiety.) For Jada, it might be missing out on an opportunity to connect with coworkers she likes. Then notice that thing, maybe the time you spend anxiously ruminating in the car. Set an intention to be mindful of this time. Repeatedly and on purpose, turn your thoughts to your physical sensations and then to what your senses are taking in from your surroundings. This will move you out of autopilot so you can live your life fully and enjoy the ride.

Takeaways

You are now equipped with a deeper understanding of your mind-body connection, your bodymind. In this chapter, you've learned that:

- Anxiety manifests itself in your body to keep you physically trapped.
- You can experience anxiety in any part of your body. The way you feel anxiety is different from how others feel it.
- Our thoughts and emotions are experienced in the brain, the gut, and the immune system, which explains why anxiety is so all-encompassing.
- Increasing self-awareness is the first important step in reducing anxiety's harmful effects on your body.
- Mindful movement, such as yoga, unites your mind and body so you can approach your anxiety with your entire self.
- As you increase your awareness and live mindfully, you can shift out of autopilot and begin living your life fully, with purpose and intention.

Use this knowledge to connect with your true self and identify exactly how anxiety is disrupting your well-being. Then target your symptoms to effectively untangle yourself.

Mindful Moment—Scan Your Body to Notice What It's Up To

Sit or lie down comfortably. Draw in a breath and turn your attention to the sound of the air entering your body. Feel your body respond. Hold for a few seconds and note how you feel. Release your breath and notice your body respond. Now scan your body, starting at one end and working your way gradually, methodically to the other end. Without passing judgment or trying to change anything, notice what the outside of your body is experiencing. How does the air feel on your skin? Is it warm? Cool? Is it blowing across you, or is it still? How do your clothes feel against your skin? Is your mouth tense or relaxed? What are your forehead and eyebrows doing? Is your hair brushing against anything? Then return to your starting point and scan again, this time attending to what your body is up to on the inside. How are your muscles right now? Is your gut empty? Full? Gurgling? Feel your heartbeat. Can you hear it? Be fully present with your entire body, top to bottom, outside and in. When your thoughts intrude, return your attention to your body.

*I have learned over the years
that when one's mind is made up,
this diminishes fear;
knowing what must be done
does away with fear.*

—**Rosa Parks**

CHAPTER EIGHT

WEEK SEVEN:
Facing Your Fears

Anxiety and fear can be terribly unpleasant, and that's putting it mildly! Fears are not something we typically want to face. (Remember what you've learned about what the body does in response to fear, anxiety, worry, and panic—that's the body conspiring with the brain, the entire bodymind working together, to keep us out of harm's way.) Sometimes, though, we will never feel completely safe until we face "harm's way." Sometimes, the best way out of anxiety isn't around, over, or under; it's smack through the middle. That's what this chapter is all about. This week, you will intentionally (that's right—you'll choose to do it on purpose) face situations that cause you anxiety and hold you back from your life. In so doing, you'll be taking charge of your anxiety rather than continuing to be at its mercy. You'll live, and you'll thrive.

Desensitization Practice

Anxiety makes us believe that everything is dangerous and must be avoided; however, if we avoided everything that made us worried or fearful, we'd miss our lives entirely. Most things we fear aren't truly harmful. Therefore, facing them directly is often the best way to get over them so we can thrive. Confronting our fears is officially known as desensitization or habituation.

Desensitization is the practice of changing your anxious thoughts and feelings by changing your behavior. It involves repeated exposure to your fear and worry. This sounds overwhelming, but committing to it offers you numerous benefits.

When you engage in a desensitization practice, you:

- Teach your whole being that you can endure the discomfort
- See that the bad outcomes you think will happen usually aren't as realistic as they seem
- Stop avoiding
- Increase your tolerance of things that cause anxiety
- Build acceptance of anxiety so you can keep going even when you're anxious or afraid
- Survive what you fear
- Increase self-efficacy, the belief in yourself that you can do it
- Free yourself to live your life fully

You can take different approaches to desensitization. All involve facing your fears, so all can be uncomfortable and downright difficult. If you are dealing with extreme fears or phobias, it may be wise to enlist the help of a professional therapist. Many therapists are trained in exposure therapy and can guide you securely through the process.

Gradual Exposure vs. Flooding

These practices involve full immersion in your fear or anxiety. In gradual exposure, you take a slow-and-steady approach to facing your fears, confronting them in pieces rather than all at once. Flooding is just as it sounds: you flood yourself with your full fear, facing the entirety all at once. Flooding can be staged and time-limited, so that you first face your fear for just a few minutes. Then you do it again for a longer period of time. Flooding is intense and can be overwhelming, but it usually desensitizes you to your fear much faster than gradual exposure. The one that's right for you is the one that fits your personality. Are you the type of person who bites into a lemon, or do you squeeze just a drop onto your finger and lick it?

In Vivo vs. Imaginal

Gradual exposure and flooding can be done in vivo (in your life), or you can visualize your fears, confronting them in your imagination. Therapists often use a combination of the two, perhaps starting in the comfort of the office and your imagination and later stepping forth into the world. Both approaches are equally powerful. Visualizing your fears can be as real as facing them in life. Think of how powerful your thoughts are and how convincing anxiety can be in your mind. You can turn the tables on anxiety by imagining your fears, picturing yourself facing them, and getting used to them so that they no longer have power over you.

Interoceptive

Interoceptive exposure is an internal process that involves facing your fear of your physical symptoms of anxiety, like the chest pains that mimic a heart attack or the light-headedness that makes people afraid to venture out in public lest they faint. If you are bothered by your physical reactions to fear, interoceptive exposure can help by dulling you to the sensations. Here, you trigger your symptoms, such as by hyperventilating, running in place, or spinning to induce dizziness, shortness of breath, and rapid heartbeat. Once you feel the sensations, you pay attention to them and notice that you are actually okay.

Fear Hierarchy

A fear hierarchy, sometimes called a desensitization hierarchy, is a useful tool in any type of exposure therapy. When anxiety and fear loom large, it can be hard to know where to start. Create a fear hierarchy by brainstorming your fears. Then, when they're out in front of you, list them from least to most anxiety-provoking. Now you have an order in which to approach your fears. Start with exposure to what bothers you the least and work your way up this anxiety ladder. One by one, you'll become desensitized, thus knocking fears down.

Exposure to Your Fears

To begin, create a fear hierarchy, and choose a fear that ranks low on your list. Over time, when you have engaged in this exercise enough that you have become accustomed to this fear (it no longer causes you anxiety), move up to the next fear and practice this exercise again.

1. Settle into a favorite chair, and wiggle around to get comfortable. Notice how your body feels.
2. Take slow, deep breaths in and out, and feel your body expand and relax with each breath.

3. Choose an object or a point in the room on which to focus, and use it to ground yourself in this moment. Notice its details and simply observe them. Reassure yourself that if your anxiety spikes during this exercise, you can simply open your eyes and refocus on the object as a reminder that you're safe in your present moment.
4. Close your eyes and continue to breathe slowly and deeply.
5. Visualize the fear you've chosen to get used to and diminish.
6. Be mindful of your thoughts, emotions, and physical sensations; notice them without judging them.
7. Continue to focus on the image of your fear. Stay with it despite your anxiety.
8. Repeat these mantras to yourself, slowly and calmly: "I am aware of my fear. I am aware that my reactions don't mean I'm in danger. I breathe through my fear. I release my fear."
9. Visualize your fear as a giant white, fuzzy dandelion puff. Inhale deeply, and as you exhale, blow it away, enjoying it breaking apart and blowing away.
10. Open your eyes, and as you continue to breathe, refocus on your centering object or point in the room.
11. Mindfully notice your body and mind become calm.

Do this mindfulness and desensitization exercise often to reduce the strength and power of your fears.

Why Exposure Therapy Works

By facing your fears on purpose, you become desensitized to them, habituated, so used to them that you stop automatically reacting to them out of habit. It's like reading a captivating book for the first time. As you read, you are enthralled. The pages practically turn themselves, and you are surprised at every turn, enraptured until the end. You want to read it again, and eventually you do. The second time, you're still emotionally involved, but you're not quite as surprised by all the twists and turns of the plot. If you read it a third time, you might still like the story and the characters, but you're not as attached. Read it a fourth time, and you might become bored and disenchanted, never to open that book again.

This is what happens when you habituate your anxiety and fears. You keep reading your fearsome horror story again and again so that eventually you become bored and disenchanted. To help you see the process through, keep in mind that anxiety's stories are largely fiction, exaggerated tales that don't actually harm you in your real world. Believing anxiety's tales and being trapped by them is what's harmful, so examine the pages and finally close the book on anxiety.

Facing Your Fears

While it goes against our fight-or-flight instinct, facing our fears is a far more effective method to eradicate them than is running from them, hiding, or otherwise avoiding them. It is in pausing and allowing yourself to experience them that you gain power over them. When you're in control, you choose your thoughts, emotions, and behavior. Fear and anxiety no longer decide for you.

Mindfulness is a vital component to facing your fears. When you become desensitized or habituated to a fear, your gut reaction (anxiety and all its symptoms and effects) diminishes because you're paying less attention to it. This is partially because you're growing accustomed to your fear and it's becoming boring. To make exposure therapy even more successful in your life, it's important to shift and to replace your focus. Instead of paying attention to your anxiety, notice your real life in your present moment. With mindfulness, you have the power of choice. You select what you pay attention to. Perhaps you carry a focus object with you to pull your attention out of your fearful thoughts and onto the item. Or maybe you tune in to your surroundings—looking, listening, feeling, smelling, and completely experiencing the moment. Whatever is in your moment, you have better things to pay attention to than your fears.

When you face your fears rather than avoid them, you give yourself the power of choice. You're not at the mercy of your anxiety, and you don't have to remain a prisoner of anxious reactions.

Exposure Obstacles

Exposure therapy is challenging and stressful. If facing our fears was easy, everyone would automatically do it, and fear wouldn't exist. Instead, it's tough. It requires determination and resolve and a willingness to let yourself be afraid—on purpose. If you didn't have these qualities, you wouldn't have picked up this book, and you certainly wouldn't have made this much progress. It takes guts to stand up to anxiety. Remind yourself of this, and do a little celebration to acknowledge your strength and accomplishments.

No matter how much determination and strength you have, you might face obstacles during your exposure practice, whether you're desensitizing on your own or with a therapist. Common roadblocks that block people's progress in exposure therapy involve tackling situations that are too overwhelming and engaging in desensitization exercises without anxiety decreasing.

You started with a situation that is too overwhelming. It's understandable. You're eager to break free from the shackles of your fear, you're motivated, you believe in yourself, so you decide to tackle a big fear rather than wasting time with little fears that are manageable and not all that bothersome. But starting out with smaller fears isn't a waste of time. It's an important step that helps you become accustomed to the process of habituation in a way that feels somewhat safe. When you start small, it's easier to confront and face a fear, and you experience success that serves as a confidence boost and momentum that will carry you to the next fear you want to tackle. If you start with something too intimidating, your avoidance reaction kicks in, often without you fully realizing it. Consequently, you hold back and buffer yourself from the fear, only experiencing it partially. When this happens, anxiety stays in control and prevents you from facing what you need to face in order to move on.

Your level of anxiety hasn't subsided. If you find that even smaller fears are stubbornly hanging on, take a look at how you're practicing exposure exercises. If the duration of an exercise is too short or you're not practicing often enough, your fear has opportunities to regrow. Fear is like a weed with deep roots. If you simply and quickly pluck off the part that is visible, the plant will regrow. It takes patience, time, and a willingness to dig deep to pull it out by its roots.

Above all, be kind to yourself during this process, especially in the face of obstacles. It can be downright scary to allow yourself to experience something that makes you extremely anxious. Initially, because you are finally facing something you've been avoiding for a long time, your anxiety might increase. Rather than berating yourself for the time it is taking, acknowledge your work and notice little victories. Catch yourself thinking about a fear and feeling slightly less anxious. That's the kind of progress that ultimately leads to habituation.

Takeaways

This week might have been uncomfortable, but by actively doing the work and facing your fears, you've developed a powerful tool that will help you diminish your fears so much that they will no longer bother you. You learned about exposure therapy as a way of minimizing anxiety.

- Desensitization, or habituation, involves repeated exposure to a fear so that you become used to it and no longer react anxiously.
- Different approaches to exposure therapy allow you to choose the method that's right for you: gradual or flooding, in vivo or imaginal, and interoceptive.
- Creating a fear hierarchy lets you approach your fears systematically, starting with the least intimidating.
- Mindfulness, with its emphasis on remaining present and choosing your focus, is an integral part of exposure therapy.
- Facing your fears and getting used to them is a challenging process, and you might face obstacles. Finding a balance between too easy and too overwhelming will help you find success.

Mindful Moment—Colorful Music

This exercise is helpful anytime you feel tired and wired from anxiety, fear, or worry. If you're too exhausted to exercise but need to release tension, mindfully experience colorful music. Grab a coloring book, blank sheets of paper, a paint-by-numbers set, or some flat rocks plus crayons, markers, or paint and brushes. Turn on some favorite tunes, preferably upbeat with a fast tempo, and color or paint to the beat. If you want to fully experience your sense of touch, try finger painting. Stay in your moment by acknowledging anxious thoughts that intrude and then returning your attention to your colorful music.

When we have tension in our body,
we can't sleep well or eat well.
Mindfulness of breathing can
help us relax and bring
peace to our body.
We take care of our body first.
We can take care of our mind later.

—Thich Nhat Hanh

CHAPTER NINE

WEEK EIGHT:
Practicing Relaxation

Anxiety overrides what your body is naturally designed to do. Your mind and body instinctively know how to exist calmly and to operate in smooth balance, but anxiety interferes and prevents you from experiencing well-being. As you've worked through this book, week by week, you've been learning to supersede anxiety and take back control. This week, you'll be adding a final component, one that works in harmony with the others. You're about to learn how to induce your body's existing relaxation response.

This chapter is about much more than me telling you to relax. How many times have you had someone tell you, "Just relax! Everything will be fine"? I never appreciated hearing that, because if it were that simple, of course I'd just relax. You might feel the same way. This chapter will take you beyond that to show you how to relax. You'll be learning some specific, research-based relaxation techniques to help your body do what it already knows how to do: calm down, rest, and reset.

The Relaxation Approach

Purposeful relaxation approaches are techniques we choose to do to help our mind and body do what they need to do to keep us untangled from anxiety and stress. Structured, intentional relaxation is a way of tuning in to our bodies to increase our awareness of our inner workings. When we're aware that our body and mind are reacting to anxiety and stress, we can step in and help ourselves return to our natural, tension-free state. Therapeutic relaxation techniques have been around for thousands of years. Perhaps the oldest such approach is meditation, including mindfulness. Other forms of relaxation therapy are more recent. A doctor by the name of Edmund Jacobson developed Jacobson's relaxation technique in the 1920s to help his patients better deal with anxiety (today, the technique is usually called progressive muscle relaxation). In 1979, Jon Kabat-Zinn created his mindfulness-based stress-reduction program at the University of Massachusetts. Modern techniques build on the ancient; together, they help us help ourselves to regulate and balance.

Therapeutic relaxation is supported by research. The techniques in this chapter have been designed to decrease physical and mental stress, anxiety, and tension, and they work. In a 2001 study published in *Western Journal of Medicine*, Andrew Vickers and his colleagues examined evidence from a variety of randomized trials and concluded that formal relaxation techniques effectively reduce anxiety, especially anxiety associated with stressful situations. Another study, appearing in *Biological Psychology* in 2002, demonstrated that a technique called abbreviated progressive muscle relaxation training positively impacts brain and body by decreasing cortisol, lowering heart rate, and reducing the subjective experience of anxiety and stress.

One reason relaxation techniques are so effective is that, like anxiety, they are all-encompassing. They seek and find anxiety wherever you're experiencing it in your bodymind, and they gently oust it by helping you let go of stress and tension. Relaxation involves:

- Quieting the mind (but not emptying it of thoughts and feelings, for this isn't possible)
- Allowing our thoughts to just flow in and out naturally, without us getting stuck in them (anxious thoughts can pop up, but we don't latch on to them)
- Focusing attention
- Pausing, breathing, connecting to the moment and to yourself as a whole, and healing

When we practice relaxation, we positively impact our entire body-mind. Thoughts decelerate, muscle tension decreases, breathing slows and becomes deeper and more regular, and heart rate and blood pressure decrease. Relaxation allows us to change how our nervous system is functioning. (That's right—we aren't passive bystanders of our body's functions but can intentionally affect them.) Anxiety and stress activate the sympathetic nervous system and keep it perpetually revved up so that we're in a constant state of agitation. Our fight-or-flight response stays on because the brain and body continually produce and release stress hormones like cortisol, norepinephrine, and adrenaline. When we intervene with relaxation techniques, we turn off the sympathetic nervous system and turn on the parasympathetic nervous system, the "rest-and-digest" response. Then, instead of stress hormones dominating, other chemicals, like the neurotransmitter gamma aminobutyric acid, or GABA (known as the brain's tranquilizer), take over. The brain's electrical activity is soothed, and slow-cycling brain waves become prominent.

Before diving into some relaxation exercises, reflect for a moment on this question: Why do you want to relax? While therapeutic relaxation won't eliminate stressors and problems, it will help you live your life calmly and well despite them. If you want to relax so you can feel whole, regain your enthusiasm for your life, develop peace of mind, and replace anxiety with well-being, then sit back, get comfortable, become aware, and, well, relax.

Relax Yourself

The exercises you're about to do are based on three prominent relaxation techniques: deep relaxation, muscle relaxation, and visualization and guided imagery. Over the course of the week, try them all more than once to see if you notice one that works better for you than others. Everyone is different, so we all have different experiences with these exercises.

You can take two approaches to relaxation exercises; typically, people use both rather than choosing one over the other:

- Develop a daily relaxation ritual. Choose a space in your home and make it comfortable and inviting. Spend some time each day, even just 5 or 10 minutes, engaging in a relaxation technique. This keeps your body balanced over time and trains your parasympathetic nervous system to assert itself over your sympathetic nervous system.
- Engage in a relaxation technique, even if it's modified and brief, the moment you become aware that you're anxious and stressed. Wherever you are, do one of these exercises in its entirety or adapt it to the moment by selecting components such as deep breathing and subtly tensing and relaxing your muscles.

Deep breathing is the foundation of each of the following techniques. This is great news, because you already know how to breathe. Your body really does know what to do. You just need to help it out a bit.

Deep Relaxation

Meditation induces a state of deep relaxation by slowing you down completely, from your automatic bodily operations to your conscious thoughts. It doesn't require a monastery or fancy equipment—not even a meditation cushion. It is as simple as focusing on one thing, such as your breath, an object in your hand, or a spot on the wall across from you. ("Simple" isn't the same as "easy," so be patient with yourself when your thoughts keep wandering.)

Set a timer to chime gently after five minutes. You can meditate longer if you wish. Position yourself so that you are comfortable enough not to be distracted by pain but not so comfortable that you instantly fall asleep. (If you fall asleep, like I sometimes do when meditating, that just means your body needs the rest and you've relaxed enough to provide it. Accept it when this happens.) Pay attention to your focal point and notice your breaths. You can say, "I am breathing in. I am breathing out," to establish gentle rhythm and focus. When the chime sounds, smile, stretch, and notice how you feel.

Progressive Muscle Relaxation

This is an exercise you can do when you're out and about, in a long line at the store, in a meeting at work, or any time or place you feel tense.

1. Notice your left foot. Curl your toes in your shoe, hold for several seconds, release your grip, wiggle your toes, and pay attention to the sensation.
2. Notice your right foot. Do the same thing you just did with your left.
3. Raise your left heel and pay attention to your calf. Squeeze your calf muscle, hold for a few seconds, and release.
4. Turn your attention to your right heel and calf, and repeat.
5. Squeeze, hold, and release each of your glutes, one butt cheek at a time.
6. Move to your abdomen. Squeeze your navel to your spine, hold, and let go. Again, pay attention to the sensation.
7. Make fists, first with your left hand and then with your right. Hold each one for several seconds before releasing. Wiggle your fingers to shake out remaining tension.
8. Squeeze, hold, and release your biceps, one at a time.
9. Shrug your shoulders to your ears, hold, and release. Wiggle them and roll your neck to further let go of stress.
10. Clench your jaw, hold it, and release. Move your jaw around to further relax it.

Visualization and Guided Imagery

The mind is very powerful. It can think thoughts and imagine scenarios that cause high anxiety. Likewise, you can think and imagine calming settings to significantly reduce anxiety.

You can do this or any other guided imagery exercise with or without background music. Some people prefer silence, while others enjoy nature sounds or relaxing instrumentals during guided imagery exercises.

Make yourself comfortable. Read through these prompts first, and then close your eyes and do the exercise on your own. Set a timer to chime gently after five minutes. Feel free to adjust the duration to suit you.

- Think of a place you enjoy and find peaceful.
- Make it come alive in your mind by recalling, one by one, sights, sounds, smells, and physical sensations.
- Imagine yourself there now. What are you doing? Are you strolling calmly? Sitting by a fire? Lying on a blanket and gazing at the stars?
- Picture in detail everything you see, letting your gaze linger on all the peaceful things.
- Imagine the sounds and let yourself listen to them.
- Feel your body relax into this place. There is nothing you must do, nowhere else to be.
- Let your thoughts come and go without trying to stop them or otherwise force them. When you catch yourself stuck in an anxious thought, release yourself by returning to your peaceful place.

The Other Relaxation Methods

Many forms of relaxation therapy exist to calm mind and body. This overview introduces other available options you may want to pursue. Some are designed to be used on your own, while others are done with a therapist in individual or group sessions. The most important thing isn't how you do it but instead is that you actively relax in a way that is meaningful and helpful to you.

The idea of "active relaxation" seems like an oxymoron, a concept whose words contradict each other. Believe it or not, relaxation is an activity that requires work. In our fast-paced society, relaxation is something we humans have lost sight of. We're out of touch with our bodymind's need for downtime, and we're out of practice.

Happily, there are tried-and-true, proven relaxation methods available to help guide you. All can be enhanced by doing them mindfully, with your full attention on how you feel during the activity. Also, breathing slowly and deeply during relaxation exercises deepens the experience. Like the entire process of reducing anxiety, learning how to relax takes practice. After reading about each of these approaches, you might consider selecting one that resonates with you and beginning your relaxation journey there. Give yourself time to get used to it, and feel free to personalize it, adding or subtracting different elements to make it the most effective for you. You can add other methods, too. Find what works for you, and actively embrace it to live calmly and peacefully despite the stress, anxieties, and other challenges of life.

SELF-HYPNOSIS

This approach begins in a therapy session with a professional trained in hypnotherapy. After generating relaxation, the therapist gives you a code word that you subconsciously associate with the state of relaxation. Then you can use the code word on your own to enter self-hypnosis and a state of relaxation.

AUTOGENIC TRAINING

Autogenic relaxation is the process of entering a state of deep physical relaxation. In a group or individual therapy session, you learn the process of creating a sense of heaviness and warmth in each part of your body. As you release tension and anxiety, your entire body slows down and lets go.

BIOFEEDBACK

This painless procedure puts you in touch with your body to help you develop awareness of your physical responses to anxiety. Using electrodes and monitors, you see how certain functions like heart rate, blood pressure, and even brain waves respond to stress and relaxation. Increased awareness leads to quicker action to replace anxiety with relaxation.

YOGA

Yoga means union of mind, body, and spirit. Through mindful, flowing movements, poses, and stretches, you relax your body and calm your mind. Tai chi and qigong are other similar approaches that use movement to relax body and mind.

MUSIC

Playing instruments, singing, and listening to music are extremely therapeutic. Music therapy involves working with a therapist, in a group or individually, to reduce anxiety with rhythm and sound. Relaxing with music can easily be done on your own, too, by settling in with soothing music and letting waves of calm wash through you.

MINDFULNESS-BASED STRESS REDUCTION (MBSR)

A formal program conducted by trained professionals, MBSR is offered nationwide at hospitals, clinics, and universities. Participants learn mindfulness, meditation, yoga, and awareness of mind and body to reduce stress, anxiety, and even chronic pain.

AROMATHERAPY

Rather than a formal method, this is the practice of adding scents, usually in the form of essential oils in a diffuser, to any relaxation technique you are using. Using calming oils, including but not limited to lavender, chamomile, or cedarwood, can help induce and maintain a sense of calm.

Takeaways

This week, you began helping your whole being, your entire bodymind, relax. Isn't it amazing that you have the power to slow things down that you probably didn't think you could control? If anxiety can take over your sympathetic nervous system, it makes sense that you can override it by activating your parasympathetic nervous system. You now know how to do this by using relaxation techniques such as:

- Deep relaxation (meditation)
- Muscle relaxation exercises
- Visualization and guided imagery

You can use relaxation techniques on your own, or you can work with a mental health professional to learn other guided approaches as well.

Mindful Moment—A Walk in Nature

You don't have to lie down or sit still to relax completely. Engage in a mindful walk every day to further relax your whole self. Leave your phone and other sources of stimulation and distraction behind and set off on a casual stroll. Set your own pace, one that feels natural. Pay attention to each step—the feel of your shoes on the path and your feet in your shoes. Tune in to your legs, torso, arms, shoulders, neck, and head. How do they feel? Just notice without judging. Take in everything around you with your senses. Notice and appreciate beauty. Listen for pleasant sounds, and let unpleasant sounds be a reminder that you are here, now. What scents does your nose pick up? How does the air feel on your skin? Whenever your thoughts wander to worries and stress, gently return your attention to your walk. And of course, breathe deeply as you go.

*And when things start to
happen, don't worry.
Don't stew.
Just go right along.
You'll start happening too.*

—Dr. Seuss

CHAPTER TEN

Navigating the Path Ahead

You are continuing along the wonderful, twisty, topsy-turvy path of your life. You have come far despite anxiety, and you have a long, beautiful path ahead. Look around you right now. Take everything in. Look inside yourself, too, and take that in. Don't judge a thing; just experience it. This is your path right now, the only real path there is. The old path is behind you, and you haven't yet forged your future path.

This chapter is far from the final chapter. It's a commencement, a new beginning. You are ready to live mindfully, fully present in each moment, and enjoy a sense of inner peace every step along the path ahead. While it isn't realistic to expect anxiety to be fully gone, you've learned a lot about your anxiety and have tools you can use. This final chapter will help steady you as you move ever forward.

Now you will target your unique challenges and begin to craft a plan that includes strategies for dealing with anxiety when it appears in your life. You will also discover ways you can find support for your ongoing voyage. You are empowered, so let's continue the momentum.

Your Relationship with Anxiety

You are ready to live more fully every step you take on your path, untangled from your anxiety. Anxiety will still be present, but it will be different now. You are making a new relationship with it. No longer will it control you, preventing you from participating fully in the life you want to have. It will still pop up from time to time, but you're the boss now.

I still get anxious at times, especially around perfectionism and social anxiety. However, anxiety is no longer in charge of who I am or how I live. I have learned to swiftly recognize my own unique symptoms when they occur, and I consciously choose to use the tools and techniques in this book to live my quality life even when anxiety tries to take charge. You are ready to do that, too!

Living an anxiety-free life has never been about living completely without anxiety, because that isn't humanly possible. You care about things; therefore, anxiety is going to be present. Living an anxiety-free life is about experiencing anxiety and moving forward anyway. It's about accepting that it's there without letting it overtake you. You have everything you need to do this: your breath, your senses, your awareness, your goals and values, your ability to shape your thoughts and emotions, and your power to choose your actions.

You can live in the present and be confident that you will handle whatever worries and fears you'll face on your path ahead by creating a plan to deal with continued anxiety.

Target Anxiety Challenges

Now that you've developed increased awareness of your own unique anxiety, you can use this insight to your advantage. Knowledge really is power. When you know what triggers your anxiety, how your bodymind responds to it, and what works best for you, you can craft a plan to deal with your worries and fears whenever they show up in your life.

Having a plan for anxiety means you'll be less likely to get snared and stuck. Knowing what you'll do when anxiety strikes will help prevent you from reverting to fight-or-flight mode, struggling against anxiety, or avoiding people, places, and things that cause you discomfort. Make an informed action plan to target anxiety challenges.

Understand Your Anxiety

"Anxiety" is a broad and vague term, just as "worry" is a nonspecific action. Recall what you've learned about the types of anxiety and your own experience with it (you might find it helpful to look back at chapters 1 and 2).

In your notebook, jot down situations or events that tend to trigger anxiety, certain times of day or conditions (like being tired or hungry) that lead to anxiety, and symptoms you'll be aware of to tell you that you're becoming anxious. This way, you'll stay a step ahead of anxiety and be able to minimize its negative effects.

Know What Works for You

Just as everyone's anxiety is unique, so, too, is everyone's plan to deal with it. Listen to your mind and body, experiment with different approaches, and discover what works best to calm you when you're worried or afraid. Which of the mindfulness exercises throughout the book have you found to be most helpful? Do you respond better to intense physical activity, lying down and listening to calming music, meditation, jumping into a creative project, or something else entirely? Try the various things we've explored together in this book, and add your own activities, too. The key is to try, try, and try some more, noting what reduces your anxiety the most.

Make a Plan

An anxiety plan is as simple as this: do more of what works! Here's where it gets a little tricky, though. Your worries and anxieties will change, and your responses will change as well. You might find that riding your bike usually burns away anxiety, but sometimes it doesn't. That doesn't mean you're doomed. That just means that in that moment, you need to do something else to quiet your mind and soothe your body. When you have a maintenance plan in place, you can consult it whenever you feel stuck. That way, you can keep moving forward rather than become overwhelmed by anxiety.

To create your plan, be intentional about finding what works for you. Here are some things to consider.

Find What Works for You

In having a plan to deal with anxiety, the goal isn't to write rigid rules for what you must do or not do. That can easily become as much of a trap as anxiety itself. Instead, think of this as a process, an adventure. Be open to trying new things, and record what is successful in helping you move past anxiety moment by moment. You're creating a sustainable maintenance program full of actions you can take to calm anxiety in any given moment. Many people find the following ideas helpful. Keep the ones you like and add the strategies you discover on your own to the list.

Make a List

Because no single technique eradicates every anxious thought or emotion, having many options from which to choose is useful. Keep a running list of all the things that help reduce your anxiety. This way, you can select something that speaks to you whenever you notice anxiety threatening to invade your space. Include a variety of techniques, some active, some quiet. Keep in mind that you'll be in different places, circumstances, and times of day, and include things to fit different situations. For example, you might not be able to leave work to take a mindful walk, but you can do deep-breathing exercises.

Make a Schedule

Humans need predictability to feel stable and calm. Some of us need it more than others, but we all benefit to some degree from schedules and routines. Develop a routine for your mornings, afternoons, and evenings and adhere to it as much as possible without being rigid. Schedule a time for anxiety-reducing activities. Perhaps you'd benefit from a mindful cup of coffee or tea in the morning, an afternoon run or reading time, and winding down with gentle yoga before bed. Find things that bring you joy and peace, and schedule them into your daily routine.

Choose When to Practice Mindfulness

For some people, setting aside time every day to practice mindfulness helps them feel calm and in control. Others prefer to use it whenever they catch themselves being anxious. When you're starting out with mindfulness, it's often most effective to keep your practice simple. The more you use mindfulness, the more you'll find that it becomes not a practice separate from the rest of your life but the very way you live life. It eventually becomes a state of being present, focused, and calm in each moment, no matter what that moment brings.

Choose a Setting

When you are initially building a mindful way of life, it can be useful to dedicate a special place to practice. You might select a favorite room in your home, a quiet spot in your yard, or somewhere else you feel relaxed and comfortable. Make sure it's easily accessible every day so you can set aside time to go there and simply breathe and be. Personalize your place and make it comfortable and welcoming. When you have a place to go and be mindful, often just stepping into that place causes calm to wash over you.

Create a Ritual Around Your Practice

A ritual is more than a routine. Like a routine, it's something done regularly, but it also involves a special way of doing that thing. If you enjoy making models or working with clay, create a special ritual around it to deepen the experience. Set the mood with lighting and music. Sip a favorite beverage while you work. Maybe even have a special pair of socks or slippers to wear while you're engaged in the activity. Rituals help you relax because they're pleasant and because they signal your brain that it is time to engage in your fun, anxiety-reducing activity.

Don't Restrict Yourself

Having your list of activities and a schedule for doing them is important, but remember that the idea is to generate many different ideas, so you always have something fresh to try. If you restrict yourself to just a few options, you'll eventually become bored. A bored mind is a wandering mind, and a wandering mind is not a mindful mind. When you're not engaged in what you're doing, anxiety can easily work its way in. Accept the challenge of adding to your list and trying new things.

Find Ways to Enrich Your Practice

To avoid restricting yourself, continually seek ways to enrich your mindfulness practice and anxiety-reducing plan. Explore new interests by wandering among the shelves of your library, looking through college course offerings (you don't have to sign up for courses, just see what topics pique your interest), or exploring local community centers to find classes and other activities. Adding activities to your repertoire provides new ways to practice mindfulness and replace anxious thoughts with positive, new ones.

Finding Support

You never have to go at this alone! Anxiety is part of the human condition, which means that there are so many others out there to connect with for mutual support and help. You can engage in therapy with a mental health professional, join support groups, and take courses to boost your journey. In our digital era, support is available for everyone, even if you don't have access to resources in person or if your current level of anxiety is so high that in-person connection feels overwhelming. (If you're in that position, don't dismiss in vivo connection forever. With support, you'll work your way toward participation in community groups and classes.)

Use these resources to find professional help and support groups in your community as well as to get online help.

Mental Health Therapy Finders

Seek professional help in your community by asking your primary physician for recommendations. You can also visit your library, community centers, clinics, and hospitals, as they often display pamphlets, cards, and brochures from local mental health organizations and private therapists.

Additionally, you can use online directories to locate therapists near you. These are reputable sources:

Choosing Therapy: ChoosingTherapy.com

GoodTherapy: GoodTherapy.org

Psychology Today: PsychologyToday.com/us/therapists

Online Mental Health Therapy

Online therapy is a growing industry, and for good reason. It increases access to mental health professionals and can make therapy more convenient. These are among the most reputable organizations providing online help:

BetterHelp: BetterHelp.com

MDLIVE: MDLIVE.com

Talkspace: Talkspace.com

TeenCounseling.com: TeenCounseling.com

Support Groups

Support groups are typically led by people who live with, or have lived with, anxiety rather than by mental health professionals. Support groups are different from group therapy, a type of professional mental health therapy, in that they're peer-led, are less structured (but are still highly focused on a topic such as anxiety), and are often free. In support groups, members share their own stories, exchange resources, and help each other troubleshoot problems. These resources lead you to online groups and forums as well as to directories to help you locate local in-person groups:

Anxiety Central: Find support forums for different anxiety disorders and challenges: Anxiety-Central.com

Anxiety Community: Discover forums for numerous mental health topics, including anxiety: AnxietyCommunity.com

Friends' Health Connection: Online connection and support for physical and mental health, including anxiety: FriendsHealthConnection.org

Psychology Today: Find a variety of support groups, including groups for anxiety, with Psychology Today's Support Group Finder: PsychologyToday.com/us/groups

MeetUp: MeetUp is a resource to help people connect with others for numerous different purposes. You can use this site to find anxiety and/or mindfulness groups in your area: MeetUp.com

National Alliance on Mental Illness (NAMI): Locate classes and support groups in your area: NAMI.org

Keep Going

Pause for a moment and appreciate yourself for how far you have come. Plan something simple yet special to celebrate your success!

Hopefully, you are feeling empowered. You decided that you no longer want to live tangled up in anxiety, and you acted on your decision. You've dedicated your time and energy to reading this book, and you've picked up new information, perspectives, techniques, and mindfulness activities that you can use in every moment going forward. You can make untangled living your way of being.

It's not always easy. Sometimes anxiety is strong. Sometimes you're more tired than usual, or you're hungry or thirsty or facing unusual stress. In the past, anxiety could use these things against you to take over your thoughts and emotions, and dictate what you did and didn't do. No more! You have what anxiety doesn't: the freedom and ability to choose how to respond.

Anxiety is mindless. It tries to take over your mind because it doesn't have one of its own. You are now mindful, and you will continue to develop and grow in this ability. You choose your thoughts, feelings, and behaviors. Living mindfully and untangling anxiety does take practice, patience, and persistence—all traits you clearly have because you have made it this far in the book!

Even when anxiety and fear creep in, return to your strengths and the knowledge and skills you've gained in this book. Onward and upward, through storms and sunshine!

Resources

The following collection of resources can help you further decrease your anxiety and build your mindfulness practice so it becomes a mindful, untangled way of life. Keep your journey going, and continually create your quality life!

Books

101 Ways to Stop Anxiety: Practical Exercises to Find Peace by Tanya J. Peterson

Be Calm: Proven Techniques to Stop Anxiety Now by Jill P. Weber

Break Free: Acceptance and Commitment Therapy in 3 Steps by Tanya J. Peterson

Breathwork: A 3-Week Breathing Program to Gain Clarity, Calm, and Better Health by Valerie Moselle

Calm: Calm the Mind, Change the World by Michael Acton Smith

Coming to Our Senses: Healing Ourselves and the World Through Mindfulness by Jon Kabat-Zinn

Complete Book of Mindful Living: Awareness and Meditation Practices for Living in the Present Moment by Robert Butera and Erin Byron

Declutter Your Mind: How to Stop Worrying, Relieve Anxiety, and Eliminate Negative Thinking by S. J. Scott and Barrie Davenport

The 5-Minute Anxiety Relief Journal: A Creative Way to Stop Freaking Out by Tanya J. Peterson

The Happiness Trap: How to Stop Struggling and Start Living by Russ Harris

How to Eat by Thich Nhat Hanh

How to Relax by Thich Nhat Hanh

How to Sit by Thich Nhat Hanh

How to Walk by Thich Nhat Hanh

Meditation for Relaxation: 60 Meditative Practices to Reduce Stress, Cultivate Calm, and Improve Sleep by Adam O'Neill

Mindfulness for Beginners: Reclaiming the Present Moment—and Your Life by Jon Kabat-Zinn

Mindfulness in Action: Making Friends with Yourself through Meditation and Everyday Awareness by Chögyam Trungpa

The Mindfulness Journal for Anxiety: Daily Prompts and Practices to Find Peace by Tanya J. Peterson

The Mindfulness Workbook for Anxiety: The 8-Week Solution to Help You Manage Anxiety, Worry, and Stress by Tanya J. Peterson

The Power of Now: A Guide to Spiritual Enlightenment by Eckhart Tolle

The Stress Management Workbook: De-Stress in 10 Minutes or Less by Ruth C. White

Wherever You Go, There You Are: Mindfulness Meditation in Everyday Life by Jon Kabat-Zinn

Websites

Explore these websites to gain useful help and information on general mental health and well-being, anxiety, and mindfulness.

Anxiety and Depression Association of America (ADAA): ADAA.org

Anxiety Centre: AnxietyCentre.com

Calm Clinic: CalmClinic.com

The Free Mindfulness Project: FreeMindfulness.org

HealthyPlace: HealthyPlace.com

Mindful: Mindful.org

Mindfulnet: mindfulnet.org

National Alliance on Mental Illness (NAMI): NAMI.org

Pocket Mindfulness: PocketMindfulness.com

Psych Central: PsychCentral.com

Social Anxiety Support Forum: SocialAnxietySupport.com

Apps

I've found these apps to be outstanding resources to decrease anxiety, build mindfulness, and cultivate well-being.

Calm: This app for meditation and sleep will help you reduce anxiety and stress through guided meditation, breathing programs, and classes. Some content is free, but the app requires a yearly subscription for full access.

Happify: Happify offers inspiring content, informational tracks, activities and games to help you change habits, build skills, reduce stress, and increase happiness. It's free and includes in-app purchases.

Headspace: Build meditation and mindfulness skills in a variety of life areas. Some content is free; a subscription provides full access to their courses and content.

Insight Timer: This free meditation app gives you access to a large library of free, guided meditations. If you'd like to take any of their numerous courses, you have the option to buy a membership.

References

Introduction

Campbell, Polly. "Why You Should Celebrate Everything." Psychology Today. December 2, 2015. psychologytoday.com/us/blog/imperfect-spirituality/201512/why-you-should-celebrate-everything.

Dubois-Maahs, Jessica. "Why You Should Celebrate Small Wins." Talkspace. August 1, 2018. talkspace.com/blog/why-you-should-celebrate-small-wins.

Chapter One

Abraham, Micah. "Hypnosis as a Possible Treatment for Anxiety." Calm Clinic. October 28, 2018. calmclinic.com/anxiety/treatment/hypnosis.

American Psychiatric Association. *Diagnostic and Statistical Manual of Mental Disorders, Fifth Edition* (DSM-5). Arlington, VA: American Psychological Association, 2013.

Antony, Martin M., and Karen Rowa. *Social Anxiety Disorder: Advances in Psychotherapy; Evidence-Based Practice.* Cambridge, MA: Hogrefe Publishing, 2012.

Arch, Joanna J., and Michelle G. Craske. "Laboratory Stressors in Clinically Anxious and Non-Anxious Individuals: The Moderating Role of Mindfulness." *Behaviour Research and Therapy* 48, no. 6 (2010): 495–505. doi.org/10.1016/j.brat.2010.02.005.

Aupperle, Robin L., and P. Paulus Martin. "Neural Systems Underlying Approach and Avoidance in Anxiety Disorders." *Dialogues in Clinical Neuroscience* 12, no. 4 (2010): 517–531. ncbi.nlm.nih.gov/pmc/articles/PMC3181993.

Daitch, Carolyn. *Anxiety Disorders: The Go-To Guide for Clients and Therapists.* New York: Norton, 2011.

Evans, Susan, Stephen Ferrando, Marianne Findler, Stowell Charles, Colette Smart, and Dean Haglin. "Mindfulness-Based Cognitive Therapy for Generalized Anxiety Disorder." *Mindfulness-Based Cognitive Therapy* 22, no. 4 (2008): 145–54. doi.org/10.1007/978-3-319-29866-5_13.

Farnam Street. "Homeostasis and Why We Backslide." Accessed January 8, 2020. fs.blog/2016/06/why-do-we-backslide-on-our-goals.

Golden, Philippe R., and James J. Gross. "Effects of Mindfulness Based Stress Reduction (MBSR) on Emotion Regulation in Social Anxiety Disorder." *Emotion* 10 (2010): 83–91. psycnet.apa.org/doi/10.1037 /a0018441.

Hoffman, Stefan G., Alice T. Sawyer, Ashley A. Witt., and Diana Oh. "The Effect of Mindfulness-Based Therapy on Anxiety and Depression: A Meta-Analytic Review." *Journal of Consulting and Clinical Psychology* 78, no. 2 (2010), 169–183. doi.org/10.1037/a0018555.

Johns Hopkins Medicine. "The Brain-Gut Connection." Accessed January 14, 2020. hopkinsmedicine.org/health/wellness-and-prevention/the-brain -gut-connection.

National Institute of Mental Health (NIMH). "Specific Phobia." U.S. Department of Health and Human Services. Accessed January 14, 2020. nimh.nih.gov/health/statistics/specific-phobia.shtml.

Peterson, Tanya J. "Anxiety: It's in Your Head (Your Brain!)." HealthyPlace. February 19, 2014. healthyplace.com/blogs/anxiety -schmanxiety/2014/02/anxiety-its-in-your-head-your-brain.

———. *Break Free: Acceptance and Commitment Therapy in 3 Steps—A Workbook for Overcoming Self-Doubt and Embracing Life.* Berkeley, CA: Althea Press, 2016.

———. *The Mindfulness Workbook for Anxiety: The 8-Week Solution to Help You Manage Anxiety, Worry, and Stress.* Emeryville, CA: Althea Press, 2018.

Seligman, Linda. *Theories of Counseling and Psychotherapy: Systems, Strategies, and Skills.* 2nd ed. Upper Saddle River, NJ: Pearson Merrill Prentice Hall, 2006.

Selva, Joaquín. "History of Mindfulness: From East to West and Religion to Science." PositivePsychology.com. Updated April 2, 2020. positivepsychology.com/history-of-mindfulness.

WebMD. "Biofeedback Therapy: Uses and Benefits." WebMD, October 2, 2018. webmd.com/pain-management/biofeedback-therapy-uses -benefits.

Chapter Two

Bailey, Regina. "What Does the Brain's Cerebral Cortex Do?" ThoughtCo. December 4, 2019. thoughtco.com/anatomy-of-the-brain-cerebral -cortex-373217.

The Essential Life. Pleasant Grove, UT: Total Wellness Publishing, 2018.

Hadhazy, Adam. "Think Twice: How the Gut's 'Second Brain' Influences Mood and Well-Being." *Scientific American.* February 12, 2010. scientificamerican.com/article/gut-second-brain.

Jerath, Ravinder, John W. Edry, Vernon A. Barnes, and Vandna Jerath. "Physiology of Long Pranayamic Breathing: Neural Respiratory Elements May Provide a Mechanism That Explains How Slow Deep Breathing Shifts the Autonomic Nervous System." *Medical Hypotheses* 67, no. 3 (2006): 566–71. doi.org/10.1016/j.mehy.2006.02.042.

Learning Mind. "How Theta Waves Boost Your Intuition & Creativity and How to Generate Them." Accessed January 22, 2020. learning-mind .com/theta-waves.

Martini, R., and Edwin F. Bartholomew. *Essentials of Anatomy & Physiology. 7th ed.* Upper Saddle River, NJ: Pearson, 2017.

National Alliance on Mental Illness (NAMI). "Anxiety Disorders." December 2017. nami.org/learn-more/mental-health-conditions /anxiety-disorders.

National Institute of Mental Health (NIMH). "Any Anxiety Disorder." U.S. Department of Health and Human Services National Institutes of Health. November 2017. nimh.nih.gov/health/statistics/any -anxiety-disorder.shtml.

Peterson, Tanya J. "Five Solution-Focused Ways to Beat Anxiety." HealthyPlace. June 18, 2014. healthyplace.com/blogs/anxiety -schmanxiety/2014/06/five-solution-focused-ways-to-beat-anxiety.

———. "Safety Behaviors with Social Anxiety: Helpful or Harmful?" HealthyPlace, July 26, 2018. healthyplace.com/blogs/anxiety -schmanxiety/2018/7/safety-behaviors-with-social-anxiety-helpful -or-harmful.

Seligman, Linda. *Theories of Counseling and Psychotherapy: Systems, Strategies, and Skills.* 2nd ed. Upper Saddle River, NJ: Pearson Merrill Prentice Hall, 2006.

Smithsonian. "Homo sapiens." Smithsonian National Museum of Natural History: What Does It Mean to Be Human? January 10, 2020. humanorigins.si.edu/evidence/human-fossils/species/homo-sapiens.

Chapter Three

Burns, David D. *The Feeling Good Handbook.* New York: Plume, 1999.

Colier, Nancy. "Why Our Thoughts Are Not Real: One Physical World, but Billions of Different Internal Worlds." Psychology Today. August 23, 2013. psychologytoday.com/us/blog/inviting-monkey-tea/201308/why-our-thoughts-are-not-real.

Glasser, William. *Choice Theory: A New Psychology of Personal Freedom.* New York: Harper Collins, 1998.

Hanh, Thich Nhat. "The Sunlight of Awareness." *Lion's Roar.* May 20, 2019. lionsroar.com/sunlight-awareness.

Harris, Russ. *The Happiness Trap: How to Stop Struggling and Start Living.* Boulder, CO: Trumpeter Books, 2008.

Peterson, Tanya J. *The Mindfulness Workbook for Anxiety: The 8-Week Solution to Help You Manage Anxiety, Worry, and Stress.* Emeryville, CA: Althea Press, 2018.

Chapter Four

Berenbaum, Howard, Keith Bredemeier, and Renee J. Thompson. "Intolerance of Uncertainty: Exploring Its Dimensionality and Associations with Need for Cognitive Closure, Psychopathology, and Personality." *Journal of Anxiety Disorders* 22, no. 1 (2008): 117–125. doi.org/10.1016/j.janxdis.2007.01.004.

Carleton, R. Nicholas, Donald Sharpe, and Gordon J. G. Asmundson. "Anxiety Sensitivity and Intolerance of Uncertainty: Requisites of the Fundamental Fears?" *Journal of Behavior Research and Therapy* 45, no. 10. (2007): 2307–2316. doi.org/10.1016/j.brat.2007.04.006.

Carleton, R. Nicholas, Peter J. Norton, and Gordon J. G. Asmundson. "Fearing the Unknown: A Short Version of the Intolerance of Uncertainty Scale." *Journal of Anxiety Disorders* 21, no. 1 (2007): 105–117. doi.org/10.1016/j.janxdis.2006.03.014.

Cunic, Arlin. "Intolerance of Uncertainty Therapy for Generalized Anxiety Disorder." Verywell Mind. Updated February 8, 2020. verywellmind .com/intolerance-of-uncertainty-therapy-for-gad-4134611.

Dugas, Michel J., Mark H. Freeston, and Robert Ladoucer. "Intolerance of Uncertainty and Problem Orientation in Worry." *Cognitive Therapy and Research* 21, no. 6 (1997): 593–606. doi.org/10.1023/A:1021890322153.

Kabat-Zinn, Jon. *Mindfulness for Beginners.* Boulder, CO: Sounds True, 2016.

Leahy, Robert L. "'But What if I'm THE ONE?' How Intolerance of Uncertainty Makes You Anxious." Psychology Today. May 14, 2008. psychologytoday.com/us/blog/anxiety-files/200805/what-if-im -the-one-how-intolerance-uncertainty-makes-you-anxious.

Peterson, Tanya J. *The Mindfulness Workbook for Anxiety: The 8-Week Solution to Help You Manage Anxiety, Worry, and Stress.* Emeryville, CA: Althea Press, 2018.

"Suspending Certainty and Embracing Uncertainty." University of Minnesota Earl E. Bakken Center for Spirituality & Healing. Accessed February 5, 2020. csh.umn.edu/education/focus-areas/whole-systems-healing /leadership/suspending-certainty-and-embracing-uncertainty.

Trungpa, Chögyam. *Mindfulness in Action.* Boulder, CO: Shambhala Publications, 2016.

Chapter Five

American Psychiatric Association. *Diagnostic and Statistical Manual of Mental Disorders, Fifth Edition (DSM-5).* Arlington, VA: American Psychological Association, 2013.

Aupperle, Robin L. and P. Paulus Martin. "Neural Systems Underlying Approach and Avoidance in Anxiety Disorders." *Dialogues in Clinical Neuroscience* 12, no. 4 (2010): 517–531. ncbi.nlm.nih.gov/pmc/articles /PMC3181993.

Boyes, Alice. "Avoidance Coping." Psychology Today. May 5, 2013. psychologytoday.com/us/blog/in-practice/201305/avoidance-coping.

—. "Why Avoidance Coping is the Most Important Factor in Anxiety." Psychology Today. March 5, 2013. psychologytoday.com/us/blog/in -practice/201303/why-avoidance-coping-is-the-most-important-factor -in-anxiety.

Chödrön, Pema. "How We Get Hooked and How We Get Unhooked." *Lion's Roar*. December 26, 2017. lionsroar.com/how-we-get-hooked -shenpa-and-how-we-get-unhooked.

The Essential Life. Pleasant Grove, UT: Total Wellness Publishing, 2018.

Forsyth, John P., and Georg H. Eifert. *The Mindfulness and Acceptance Workbook for Anxiety: A Guide to Breaking Free from Anxiety, Phobias, and Worry Using Acceptance and Commitment Therapy*. Oakland, CA: New Harbinger, 2007.

Hayes, Steven C., Kirk D. Strosahl, and Kelly G. Wilson. *Acceptance and Commitment Therapy: The Process and Practice of Mindful Change*. 2nd ed. New York: Guilford Press, 2011.

Hayes, Steven C. with Spencer Smith. *Get Out of Your Mind and Into Your Life: The New Acceptance and Commitment Therapy*. Oakland, CA: New Harbinger, 2005.

Kabat-Zinn, Jon. *Coming to Our Senses: Healing Ourselves and The World Through Mindfulness*. New York: Hachette Books, 2005.

—. *Mindfulness for Beginners*. Boulder, CO: Sounds True, 2016.

Peterson, Tanya J. *Break Free: Acceptance and Commitment Therapy in 3 Steps—A Workbook for Overcoming Self-Doubt and Embracing Life*. Berkeley, CA: Althea Press, 2016.

—. *The 5-Minute Anxiety Relief Journal: A Creative Way to Stop Freaking Out*. Emeryville, CA: Rockridge Press, 2019.

—. *The Mindfulness Workbook for Anxiety: The 8-Week Solution to Help You Manage Anxiety, Worry, and Stress*. Emeryville, CA: Althea Press, 2018.

Saplakoglu, Yasemin. "Why Do Smells Trigger Strong Memories?" LiveScience. December 8, 2019. livescience.com/why-smells -trigger-memories.html.

Scott, Elizabeth. "Avoidance Coping and Why it Creates Additional
Stress." Verywell Mind. Updated December 5, 2019. verywellmind
.com/avoidance-coping-and-stress-4137836.

Weber, Jill P. *Be Calm: Proven Techniques to Stop Anxiety.* Emeryville,
CA: Althea Press, 2019.

Chapter Six

Cherry, Kendra. "The Incentive Theory of Motivation." Verywell Mind.
Last modified March 4, 2020. verywellmind.com/the-incentive-theory
-of-motivation-2795382.

Clark, Alisha H. "Stop Procrastination and Eliminate Anxiety—Here's
How." National Register of Health Service Psychologists. Accessed
February 27, 2020. psychologicalscience.org/observer/why-wait-the
-science-behind-procrastination.

Cuncic, Arlin. "Tips for Dealing with Procrastination When You Have Social
Anxiety." Verywell Mind. Last modified September 30, 2019. verywellmind
.com/procrastination-and-social-anxiety-disorder-3973931.

Icahn School of Medicine at Mount Sinai. "Brain Reward Pathways."
Neuroscience Department Laboratories. Accessed February 27, 2020.
neuroscience.mssm.edu/nestler/brainRewardpathways.html.

Jaffe, Eric. "Why Wait? The Science Behind Procrastination." Association
for Psychological Science. April 2013. psychologicalscience.org
/observer/why-wait-the-science-behind-procrastination.

Schroeder, Michael O. "Is Your Chronic Procrastination Actually a
Matter of Mental Health?" *U.S. News and World Report.* August 3,
2017. health.usnews.com/wellness/mind/articles/2017-08-03
/is-your-chronic-procrastination-actually-a-matter-of-mental-health.

Seligman, Martin E. P. *Flourish.* New York: Atria Paperback, 2011.

VIA Institute on Character. "Character Strengths." Accessed February 29,
2020. viacharacter.org/character-strengths-via.

Zetlin, Melinda. "Procrastination or Anxiety? Here's How to Tell the
Difference, According to a Psychology PhD." Inc. September 23, 2019.
inc.com/minda-zetlin/procrastination-cure-fear-anxiety-self-compassion
-alice-boyes.html.

Chapter Seven

American Psychiatric Association. *Diagnostic and Statistical Manual of Mental Disorders, Fifth Edition* (DSM-5). Arlington, VA: American Psychological Association, 2013.

Anxiety and Depression Association of America (ADAA). "Irritable Bowel Syndrome (IBS)." Accessed March 1, 2020. adaa.org/understanding -anxiety/related-illnesses/irritable-bowel-syndrome-ibs.

Cherney, Kristeen. "Effects of Anxiety on the Body." Healthline. July 20, 2018. healthline.com/health/anxiety/effects-on-body#1.

Chopra, Deepak, and Rudolph E. Tanzi. *Super Genes.* New York: Harmony Books, 2015.

———. *The Healing Self.* New York: Harmony Books, 2018.

Daitch, Carolyn. *Anxiety Disorders: The Go-To Guide for Clients and Therapists.* New York: Norton, 2011.

Folk, Jim. "Anxiety Headaches, Migraines, Head Tension Symptoms." Anxiety Centre. Last modified February 21, 2020. anxietycentre.com /anxiety/symptoms/headaches-anxiety.shtml.

Harvard Medical School. "Anxiety and Physical Illness." Harvard Health Publishing. Last modified May 9. 2018. health.harvard.edu /staying-healthy/anxiety_and_physical_illness.

National Institutes of Health (NIH). "What Are the Parts of the Nervous System?" U.S. Department of Health and Human Services National Institutes of Health. Accessed March 1, 2020. nichd.nih.gov/health /topics/neuro/conditioninfo/parts.

Trungpa, Chögyam. *Mindfulness in Action.* Boulder, CO: Shambhala Publications, 2016.

Vogelzang, Nicholas J., Aartjan T. F. Beekman, P. DeJonge, and Brenda W. J. H. Penninx. "Anxiety Disorders and Inflammation in a Large Adult Cohort." *Translational Psychiatry* 3, no. 4, e249 (April 2013). doi.org/10.1038/tp.2013.27.

Chapter Eight

Cherry, Kendra. "When and Why Does Habituation Occur?" Verywell Mind. Last modified September 30, 2019. verywellmind.com /procrastination-and-social-anxiety-disorder-3973931.

Cuncic, Arlin. *The Anxiety Workbook*. Berkeley, CA: Althea Press, 2017.

Daitch, Carolyn. *Anxiety Disorders: The Go-To Guide for Clients and Therapists*. New York: Norton, 2011.

Day, Susan X. *Theory and Design in Counseling and Psychotherapy*. Boston: Lahaska Press, 2004.

Peterson, Tanya J. *The Mindfulness Workbook for Anxiety: The 8-Week Solution to Help You Manage Anxiety, Worry, and Stress*. Emeryville, CA: Althea Press, 2018.

Seligman, Linda. *Theories of Counseling and Psychotherapy*. Upper Saddle River, NJ: Pearson Prentice Hall, 2006.

Stoddard, Jill A., and Niloofar Afari. *The Big Book of ACT Metaphors: A Practitioner's Guide to Experiential Exercises & Metaphors in Acceptance & Commitment Therapy*. Oakland, CA: New Harbinger Publications, 2014.

Chapter Nine

Brogaard, Berit. "How Deep Relaxation Affects Brain Chemistry." Psychology Today. March 31, 2015. psychologytoday.com/us/blog/the-mysteries -love/201503/how-deep-relaxation-affects-brain-chemistry.

Goldman, Rena. "What is Jacobsen's Relaxation Technique?" Healthline. May 2, 2017. healthline.com/health/what-is-jacobson-relaxation -technique.

GoodTherapy. "Autogenic Training." Updated September 23, 2016. goodtherapy.org/learn-about-therapy/types/autogenic-training.

GoodTherapy. "Relaxation." Updated June 7, 2019. relaxationtherapy.pro /index.html.

Hanh, Thich Nhat. *How to Relax*. Berkeley, CA: Parallax Press, 2015.

Kabat-Zinn, Jon. *Mindfulness for Beginners*. Boulder, CO: Sounds True, 2016.

Mulry, Reaume C. "About Relaxation Therapy: The Original Relaxation Therapy." Relaxation Therapy. Accessed March 15, 2020. relaxationtherapy.pro/index.html.

National Center for Complementary and Integrative Health (NCCIH). "Relaxation Techniques for Health." U.S. Department of Health and Human Services National Institutes of Health. Last modified May 2016. nccih.nih.gov/health/stress/relaxation.htm.

Pawlow, Laura A., and Gary E. Jones. "The Impact of Abbreviated Progressive Muscle Relaxation on Salivary Cortisol." *Biological Psychology* 60, no. 1 (2002): 1–16. doi.org/10.1016/S0301-0511(02)00010-8.

Vickers, Andrew, Catherine Zollman, and David K. Payne. "Hypnosis and Relaxation Therapies." *Western Journal of Medicine* 175, no. 4 (2001): 269–272. ncbi.nlm.nih.gov/pmc/articles/PMC1071579.

Index

Catastrophizing, 36, 47, 52, 68, 69

Celebrating, importance of, 14, 65, 96, 118

Chödrön, Pema, 59

Choice as a factor in responding to anxiety, 51, 56

Choking sensations and difficulty swallowing, 81

Chopra, Deepak, 79, 82

Cognitive behavioral therapy (CBT), 11, 16, 36, 39

Compassion. *See* Self-compassion

Cortisol, stress as releasing, 3, 24, 102, 103

Counteract a Thought exercise, 39–40

D

Daily routine, establishing, 114

Deep breathing
anxiety reactions, controlling with, 17, 114
cerebral cortex, impact on, 27
as foundational, 104
fretting, as an aid to moving away from, 75
as a mindfulness activity, 13
monkey mind, stilling with, 41
overwhelming emotions, as helping to calm, 60
as a relaxation technique, 64

Delegation, learning skill of, 72–73

Depression, 13, 14

Descartes, René, 35

Desensitization practice
choice, facing your fears resulting in, 95
common roadblocks, 96–97
Exposure to Your Fears exercise, 93–94
repeated exposure, as featuring, 91, 98
In vivo *vs.* imaginal exposure, 92–93, 98

Detachment of Thoughts exercise, 40

Diagnostic and Statistical Manual of Mental Disorders (DSM-5), 1–2, 4

Dizziness and light-headedness, 2, 6, 80, 93

Dopamine release, 72

E

Education anxieties, 29

Evaluation of Thoughts exercise, 40

Everyday responsibility anxieties, 30

Expectations, tempering, 71–72

Exposure therapy, 91–95, 96–97, 98

F

Fatigue, anxiety as cause of, 2, 81

Fear
anxiety and excessive fear, 1, 56, 63
chemical and electrical signals, as comprising, 79
everyday responsibilities, fear as disrupting, 30
exposure therapy as treating, 93–94, 95
failure, fear of, 68–69, 73, 77
fear hierarchy, 93, 98
mindfulness as counteracting, 28
negative thoughts as underlying, 35
of new situations, 49
phobias, manifesting as, 4, 6, 8, 18, 24, 92
in Self-Assessment checklist, 8

Fight-or-flight response
action plan, forestalling via, 112
avoidance, role in, 55–56
blockages, resulting in, 30
facing your fears as going against instinct, 95
as inborn programming, 38, 55
panic attacks, as preparing the body for, 62
phobias, triggering, 6, 24
reptilian brain, as responsible for, 3
sympathetic nervous system, associated with, 27, 103
uncertainty as a trigger, 46

Flooding as a desensitization technique, 92

G

Gamma aminobutyric acid (GABA), 103

Generalized anxiety, 5, 18, 22–23

Generalized anxiety disorder (GAD), 11

Gradual exposure practice, 92, 98

Guided imagery, 17, 103, 105–106, 109

Guilt, 68, 73

H

Habits, 51, 56, 70, 77

Habituation. *See* Desensitization

Worry (*continued*)

notebook prompt, 59

panic attacks, excessive worry as part of, 6, 63

as paralyzing, 73, 77

physical illness, triggering, 29, 81

prefrontal cortex, keeping one stuck in worries, 3

procrastination as a factor in, 68, 70, 73

projects, putting off worry during, 71–72

in Self-Assessment checklist, 8

selfishness, worry over indulging in, 9

as a symptom of anxiety, 1, 5, 18, 25–26

thought patterns underlying, 35, 39

Worry Time technique for reducing, 41

worry triggers, 74–75

Y

Yoga, 26, 83–84, 88, 108, 114

About the Author

Tanya J. Peterson, MS, NCC, draws from her previous experience as a high school teacher and board-certified counselor, as well as from personal experience, to write books that help people empower themselves to both reduce obstacles like anxiety and move forward despite them to create a quality life. Tanya also writes extensively for the mental health website HealthyPlace. com, including the weekly *Anxiety-Schmanxiety* blog, has posts on the Mighty, and is a regular contributor to the website Choosing Therapy. Connect with her on social media through her website, TanyaJPeterson.com.